PROBLEMS IN CIVILIZATION

ELIZABETH I

David H. Pinkney,
General Editor

PROBLEMS IN CIVILIZATION

ELIZABETH I

Edited with
an Introduction by

Lacey Baldwin Smith

Northwestern University

FORUM PRESS

Published simultaneously in Canada.

Printed in the United States of America.

Library of Congress Catalog Card Number; 79-54031

ISBN: 0-88273-407-5

Elizabeth I

—Photo courtesy of the National Portrait
Gallery, London

CONTENTS

III. ANOTHER PERSPECTIVE: WORKING WITH GLORIANA

IV. THE BENEFIT OF HINDSIGHT: THE HISTORIANS SPEAK

INTRODUCTION

O N THE FACE of it, John Knox, that outspoken and abrasive Protestant Moses of Scotland, appeared to be quite right: during the middle decades of the sixteenth century there seemed indeed to be a "monstrous regiment of women" whom God had inflicted upon a world which should by all that was natural and holy have been ruled by men. In Scotland there was a female regent, Mary of Guise (1515-1560), widow of James V, and later that tragic *femme fatale* of Europe, Mary Stuart Queen of Scots (1542-1587), who could never disentangle her sex life from the requirements of politics and royalty. In France authority was wielded by a plump Italian lady who loved dynastic intrigue and bedroom politics, Catherine de Medici (1519-1589), the regent and queen mother. And in England, three women held the scepter in rapid succession: Lady Jane Grey (1537-1554), the uncrowned nine-day queen; Mary Tudor (1516-1558), whose lot in history has been to live chained to the epithet of "bloody," and finally Elizabeth (1553-1603), who was to prove the single exception to a rule that almost every sixteenth-century male knew as a certainty: women were "weak, frail, impatient, feeble and foolish," and quite "void of the spirit of council."

On Elizabeth's succession on November 17, 1558, the Spanish Ambassador predicted nothing but trouble for a kingdom ruled by a woman (see p. 3). He might also have remarked that Elizabeth Tudor's chances of surviving were not great, to say nothing of her reigning for forty years, to win the accolades of four centuries of history by proving that success can be born of the most unlikely ingredients—indecision, old-fashioned ideas, prevarication, procrastination and inactivity. Elizabeth was the second daughter of Henry VIII, and her birth on September 7, 1533 was a bitter disappointment and source of embarrassment for her father. The baby girl, who by all rights should have been a boy, was inexorably tied to the Protestant Reformation, for Henry VIII had broken with Rome, established the independent Church of England, and launched the kingdom upon the path of Protestantism for a host of reasons—some personal, some sexual, some political, some psychological. All these reasons, however, were directly related to Henry's divorcing his first wife, Catherine of Aragon, and his marrying Anne Boleyn in order to beget a male heir. When Anne failed in her manifest duty of producing a son for her royal husband, she was discarded and executed, and her baby daughter dropped into obscurity, branded as illegitimate in the eyes of the Catholic world. Eventually, Henry VIII sired a legitimate male heir by his third wife Jane Seymour; and we know singularly little about Elizabeth Tudor after the birth of Edward in 1536, for she was no longer of historical interest since no one expected her to succeed to the throne. We know only that she endured a childhood filled with political and religious uncertainty, punctuated with four stepmothers.

When Henry VIII died in 1547, his last will and testament settled the succession on the basis of strict blood relationship without reference to the religious or marital problems of his reign: first in line was his nine-year-old son Edward VI; then his elder daughter Mary by his Catholic wife, Catherine of Aragon; and finally Elizabeth, the offspring of his tragic and portentous union with Anne Boleyn. When the old king died, Elizabeth was not yet fourteen, but she was old enough to fulfill the function reserved for all ladies of royal birth—to act as a dynastic pawn in the hands of the men who determined the fate of the kingdom. Under

Elizabeth

Edward she was almost destroyed by the political and marital ambitions of her step-uncle Thomas Seymour, who sought to use her in unseating his brother, the Duke of Somerset, who ruled the kingdom as Lord Protector and governor of the young king. Later in the reign, as her brother lay dying, Elizabeth survived the abortive palace revolution which attempted to upset Henry VIII's will and replace Catholic Mary with her Protestant cousin Lady Jane Grey. And finally, under her sister (much to Elizabeth's surprise, as well as that of most contemporary observers), she escaped the axe, for as Anne Boleyn's daughter and heir presumptive to the throne Elizabeth was a constant threat to her sister's passionate efforts to return her erring land to the Roman Catholic Church.

Despite the odds, she survived. There was no Catholic upheaval to prevent her succession, no intervention on the part of France to install the only other potential Catholic claimant to the throne, her first–cousin–once–removed, Mary Queen of Scots, who was half French and married to the Dauphin of France. Even so, the prognostications were not good in November of 1558; nor did the young Queen do much to allay the fears of those who maintained that not much could be "expected from a country governed by a Queen." Mary had proved the male chauvinists to be correct—that a woman ruler of necessity was "inconstant, variable, cruel"—for she had led her country into the humiliating marriage with Philip of Spain and the disastrous war with France. Now, under Elizabeth it looked as if the new sovereign might do even worse, for she showed signs of allowing sex to befuddle her political judgment in much the same way as religion had affected her sister's.

The Queen's privy chambers were dominated during the early years of her reign by Robert Dudley (1532-1589), third son of the Duke of Northumberland, who had been executed by Mary for his abortive attempt to change the

succession and install Lady Jane Grey. Dudley, her "Robin," was young and sexually attractive, and he introduced into court politics something that had never before existed: the male favorite who via the boudoir could influence state policy. How involved Elizabeth was with her young gallant we shall never know, but she lavished upon him the fruits of high office and the patronage of her crown. He became Master of the Horse in 1558; joined the Queen's council in 1561; was presented the following year with the monopoly of the import and export of sweet wines, which amounted to over a thousand pounds annually in an age that accounted three pounds a year a living wage; and in 1564 was created Earl of Leicester. Dudley's influence, however, was more than balanced by an industrious social parvenu, William Cecil (1520-1598), who by hard work and devotion became indispensable to the Queen first as her Principal Secretary and then, in 1571, as Lord Treasurer, when he was elevated to the peerage as Lord Burghley.

Somehow Elizabeth weathered those early years. With the help of Cecil, she worked out a religious compromise between bigoted Catholics of the old school and straight-laced Protestants of the new school, and picked up the military and diplomatic pieces from her sister's reign. She negotiated a degrading peace with France, in which the loss of England's last continental foothold, the port of Calais, had to be recognized, and she learned not to mix love with politics. As it was she was swept up in the scandal and mystery surrounding the death of Robert Dudley's first wife, and the entire court lived in fear that she might indeed marry the handsome widower. But weather those early years she did, working out a religious compromise which, instead of antagonizing everyone, miraculously satisfied enough people to make it a viable solution to the problems of the Reformation. The language of the Elizabethan religious settlement was so befuddled and obscure that, though the spirit was clearly Protestant and the Queen bore the title of Supreme Governor in defiance of Rome, the phraseology was sufficiently Catholic to ease the consciences of those subjects who deemed themselves to be more English than papist.

For a decade, until 1568, Elizabeth seemed to be supremely lucky. France was wracked by civil and religious war, in part brought on by the quick succession of four kings: Henry II, who was killed in a jousting accident in 1559; and his three sons—Francis II, who survived only a year, dying of a abscessed ear; Charles IX, who did as his mother told him; and Henry III, who succeeded to the throne in 1574 and was assassinated fourteen years later. Scotland, England's northern neighbor, was torn apart by Catholic-Protestant controversy, which was carefully fostered by William Cecil, partly to neutralize Scotland as a threat to England's back door and partly to ensure the triumph of a religious party favorable to the Protestant regime in England. And in Spain, the Catholic colossus was expending his time, energy and the wealth of the New World to defend Europe and his Mediterranean possessions from the threat of the Infidel. Philip II had no time for his sister-in-law in England. He regretted the death of his first wife, Mary Tudor, and the succession of her Protestant sister, if only because he could no longer rely on England as an ally in the long duel with France. He had to suffer in silence while his sister-in-law took her kingdom out of the Roman Catholic fold, for his only alternative was to defend the claims of Mary Stuart, who, for the time being at least, appeared to be considerably more French than Catholic. And so Elizabeth Tudor, the Protestant "bastard" of Henry VIII, was allowed to establish herself and her style of government upon the throne of England. She was young; there was time for marriage and time to establish the Tudor dynasty by the birth of an heir. After twelve years of religious, economic and political chaos under Edward VI and Mary, most people were willing to accept their new sovereign for what she was: a highly intelligent, extremely well-educated lady of twenty-five, who was extraordinarily quick in learning the art and science of kingship.

It is difficult to explain the stability of Elizabethan England, for the kingdom was exposed to all the centrifugal forces that beset France and Germany: religious fanaticism, semi-feudal loyalties, provincialism, runaway inflation, and economic and social discontent and dislocation. In part, the stability was due to the Queen's personality and style of government; the documents, descriptions and judgments incorporated in this volume of readings seek to cast light on the enigma of Gloriana's role in the making of Elizabethan England. In addition to Elizabeth herself, however, the nation's stability was also due to the structure of sixteenth-century politics and government as it operated in Tudor England. The Queen stood at the apex of a small ruling pyramid, entreé into which rested on two principles: birth and royal favor. The profits and power of government were controlled by the natural elite of society, who ranged in rank from the sixty peers in the House of Lords to the three to four thousand country gentlemen and their commercial and professional allies in trade, law and the church —the merchants, lawyers and ministers —who sat as MPs in the House of Commons and as JPs in local government.

What gave Tudor politics stability as well as dynamism was a combination of the socially indoctrinated sense of hierarchy and rank shared by all Englishmen from the Queen down to the ploughman and scullery maid, and the operation of political and economic patronage, whose chains of self-interest bound the ruling elements of England to the Tudor crown. The sovereign, in theory at least, was the custodian and bestower of all political bounty; she was also the symbol and embodiment of "degree, priority and place.'' Only by applauding and accepting in their hearts as well as in their actions the rule and semi-divinity of the monarch could the aristocratic minority maintain its own status and authority over the great unwashed majority. For example, Robert Devereux, Earl of Essex, was born to a family that could trace its lineage back fifteen generations, and in his veins flowed the blood of half the royalty of England, yet he remained a subject. Equally important, he was dependent upon the throne for his aristocratic well–being. Two key factors conditioned the operation of patronage: the natural leaders of society could not maintain the cost of their social and political position without financial support from the crown, and there were not enough offices, dignities, pensions, annuities, leases and monopolies to go around. Only by humility before authority, obedience to those in power, and friendship with someone close to the fountain of royal patronage—the Queen herself—could even a peer of the realm expect to maintain himself. William Cecil, who climbed the slippery pole of court politics and held his position next to the Queen for a lifetime, knew the secret of success: ''Be sure,'' he told his son Robert, ''to keep some great man thy friend but trouble him not for trifles.'' The formula applied to an earl as well as to a country gentleman, for behind it stood the truth of Sir Francis Bacon's statement: ''Win the Queen; if this be not the beginning, any other course I see no end.''

It was within this context that Elizabeth learned to rule; how she did it and the personal and political costs it entailedcan be read in the speeches, letters and poems of the Queen herself (see chapter II), and in the opinions of those who knew her well (see chapters I & III). By the time the ''calm and quiet season'' was over, Elizabeth had become an experienced sovereign, which was just as well, for in 1568 the domestic and international configurations changed dramatically. At home the religious extremes grew restless. Puritans clamored for further reform of the church and became increasingly paranoid over the mounting evidence that militant, international Catholicism was on the march, ready it seemed to overthrow their Queen and murder worthy Protestants in their beds. Catholics began to hearken to the Counter-Reformation, to the voices of seminary priests and Jesuits who came over to England in secrecy to revive, encourage and fortify the faith, urging citizens to place their religion above all material and political considerations.

Into this heightened religious atmosphere, on May 16, 1568, walked that ''Dragon of Discord,'' Mary Stuart Queen of Scots. Mary, as Elizabeth had already been at pains to write her (see p. 42), had not learned how to rule. After the death of her first husband, Francis II of France, in December of 1560, the eighteen-year-old widow had returned to her homeland, where she hoped to work her Stuart charm on dour Scottish lairds and on the stern morality of John Knox. Eight years, two marriages and one murder later, she was forced to abdicate in favor of her young son, James VI, and to seek asylum with her cousin, Elizabeth of England. The moment Mary arrived her presence magnified a hundredfold two problems with which Elizabeth had been coping ever since the start of her reign: the marriage issue and the succession question. The Queen had been stalling from the beginning, but in 1568 the pressure to marry, beget an heir and name a successor increased alarmingly, for the heir presumptive in the form of Mary Stuart was suddenly in England, acting as a magnet for every form of political and religious discontent. Parliament—both Lords and Commons—was determined that their Queen should marry and name a Protestant successor to the throne, lest she die and the kingdom be thrown into civil and religious war. The life expectancy of royalty was not great, and the lesson of France was close at hand. Gloriana had much to say

religious uprising

Mary's presence causing pressure

Elizabeth

on the subjects of her marriage, the succession and Mary of Scotland, and four out of the six speeches given in this book of readings deal with her refusal to do as Parliament asked, or to permit the execution of a woman who, despite the danger to herself and to her realm, was her blood cousin and legal heir to her throne.

Abroad the international situation began to deteriorate in an even more disturbing fashion. Prolonged civil and religious war in France upset the balance of military and diplomatic power upon which England's safety rested, for without France as a check to Spanish influence, Hapsburg Spain rose as the arbiter of Europe. In 1571 at the Battle of Lepanto, Philip of Spain's navy smashed the power of the Ottoman Empire, relieving Europe of the Turkish menace and permitting Philip to turn his attentions to the political and religious problems of northern Europe. Closer to home, in 1566 the economic jewel of the Spanish Empire, the Lowlands of Holland and Flanders, rose in rebellion against their Spanish master, calling upon Elizabeth to help them in their efforts to throw off the Catholic yoke. With a stricken France little more than a political cypher, with English religious sympathies and economic ties clearly in favor of the Dutch revolt, and with English commercial interests increasingly encroaching upon the Spanish monopoly in the New World, England and Spain were on a collision course, and for the next twenty-five years both at home and abroad Elizabeth faced one crisis after another.

First the northern shires, led by the semi-feudal earls of Northumberland and Westmoreland, rose in rebellion during the winter of 1569-1570. Seeking to reinstate the Catholic faith, they had been lured into treason by the presence of that catalyst for sedition, Catholic Mary Stuart. How seriously Elizabeth took the revolt and how relieved she was when her army destroyed the last of the rebels is clear in her letter to George Talbot, Earl of Shrewsbury (see p.54).

Then followed the dangerous decision to send troops into the Lowlands and thus risk open war with Spain. The Queen's council was divided on the issue, and Elizabeth delayed as long as possible, for she was not only reluctant to antagonize her brother-in-law but was also unwilling on principle to support subjects, no matter how deserving their cause, against their legal and historic ruler. It was a dangerous precedent; moreover, it was extremely expensive. For years English aid had been secret and unofficial, but in 1585 Gloriana did as William Cecil and others advised, and sent her aging favorite, the Earl of Leicester, with a force of 6,000 to the Lowlands. How changeable, difficult and irritable Elizabeth was about the entire situation is revealed in her correspondence with the Earl and with Sir Thomas Heneage (see pp. 46–48).

Finally came the inevitable: the agonizing decision to permit the execution of Mary Stuart. Cecil, Leicester, every other adviser, and the unanimous voice of Parliament all argued that the woman who persisted in conspiring the death of the Queen had to die. Elizabeth put up a prolonged fight, but on February 1, 1587, she signed her cousin's death warrant; seven days later, on order of the council, Mary was beheaded. The Queen was outraged; signing and executing she maintained were two very different things, and she vented her wrath on Cecil and the council (see pp. 63–64). Elizabeth never totally lived down her reputation for regicide. The portrait of the Queen presented by Cardinal Allen (see pp. 7–13) may be a monument to the triumph of fantasy over reality, but it depicts the contemporary image of Elizabeth in the eyes of all good Catholics.

If Gloriana was at her emotional worst over the execution of her cousin, she was at her oratorial best during the crisis of the Armada, when Philip decided that for the sake of his soul and the success of his efforts to crush the Dutch revolt, his sister-in-law would have to be dethroned, Catholicism restored, and England chastened by the might of Spain. Elizabeth's speech to her army at Tilbury in August of 1588 (see p. 37), while the Spanish Armada was still in the English Channel and the military outcome still unknown, is a marvel of showmanship and oratory.

Tilbury and the Armada—the summer and autumn of 1588—were in a sense the emotional pinnacle of the reign; thereafter came the recessional and old age, staved off by an even greater dependence on cosmetics and ritual. But despite an international war that dragged on and on, despite the strain placed on the regime by the Earl of Tyronne's rebellion in Ireland and the Earl of Essex's rebellion at home, and despite the fact that for almost ten years her court, her country and her contemporaries waited impatiently for their Queen to die, Gloriana managed to perform a miracle: she survived a decade of rather shoddy history with her reputation intact.

Even Essex's grotesque courtship with a sovereign almost twice his age, his furious denial of her divinity (see p. 68), and his final treason and execution in 1601 did not shatter the image. There were a number of handsome, witty young men at court—Sir Walter Raleigh was one until he sacrificed the Queen's favor by getting one of her maids-in-waiting with child, thus violating her strict code of sexual decorum—but Robert Devereux, Earl of Essex, was the flaming, impulsive favorite of those final years. He was Gloriana's substitute for her "Robin," the Earl of Leicester who had died in 1589, and he symbolized her refusal to make any concession to old age (see pp. 50,51). Their relationship may have had elements of grand passion, but it undoubtedly contained a grand lesson about Tudor government in general and Elizabeth Tudor in particular: no subject, no matter how mighty or how good-looking, could be permitted to question the divinity that enshrined the

Tudor throne. Whatever reality may have been during those declining years—bitter factualism at court, fawning corruption, senseless ritualism, ecomomic and political jobbery—the myth and legend prevailed: men saw, then as now, the fiction and chose to ignore reality, either out of respect for the old Queen or simply because they had been living with a myth for so long that they could no longer recognize truth when they saw it.

How then did she create the legend, manipulate, distort and somehow control reality to fit the image of her reputation? In the recital of this short biographical sketch, one thing should be apparent: Elizabeth Tudor was always the dominating figure. At the same time, it is difficult to say exactly what she did to warrant that position, except to point out that she had been born to it. Gloriana was neither theoretician nor activist. She seemed to have had no policy except to delay, obscure, and remind herself and her generation that she was Henry VIII's daughter. She never looked ahead, only backward to her father, who until her death remained her model for royalty and ruling. She detested new ideas and disapproved of the new invention called the flush toilet just as strenuously as she disliked the new cosmology of Copernicus. She resolved almost nothing during her forty–year reign, leaving to her successor (the son of her constant rival but legal heir, Mary Stuart) the job of operating an outmoded and increasingly inefficient system of government in an era of rapid economic, social, and political change. Gloriana had bid time to stand still, and, extraordinary as it seems, she succeeded. Yet no one at the time could reckon success in terms of doing nothing, for again and again one hears the refrain of those who knew her best—that nothing but disaster could be expected from a woman who was unable to make up her mind. "What her majesty will determine to do only God I think knoweth." Ever since William Cecil wrote this

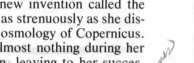

statement, historians have been posing the central question: Did Elizabeth know what she was doing? Was she the consummate politician and foresighted sovereign who sensed the supreme truth that great issues which touch men's principles and loyalties are rarely resolved, but simply replaced by other more pressing issues? Or was she supremely lucky in that time, events and William Cecil, along with other able councillors, were all on her side, sustaining her faltering steps, arguing her into rational actions, and rescuing her at the crucial moment? In other words, was Elizabeth an example of John Knox's warning that only by the "extraordinary dispensation of God's mercy" could a female ruler be saved from disaster?

The documents that follow will help to answer these questions. They will reveal a succession of personalities, portraits, and judgments. The readers will have the benefit of hindsight, of historians who have sought by research and imagination to penetrate the mystery of this woman's success (see chapter IV). But readers will also have something far more revealing: the judgment of contemporaries, those who knew, admired, hated, worked with, and suffered Gloriana; and most important of all, they will have the Queen's own words. Elizabeth will speak, but she will offer no explanation for her success. Nevertheless, she will reveal to the astute reader the qualities of her mind, the facets of her personality, the style of her operation, and possibly even the secret of the myth which she was able to maintain both in her own lifetime and in the recorded annals of history. The final picture will be neither wholly admirable nor redeeming; in all likelihood it will embody the paradox voiced by Robert Cecil, who knew Elizabeth in later life almost as well as had his father, when he noted that she was "more than a man and, in truth, something less than a woman."

GENEALOGY OF THE HOUSE OF TUDOR 1485-1603

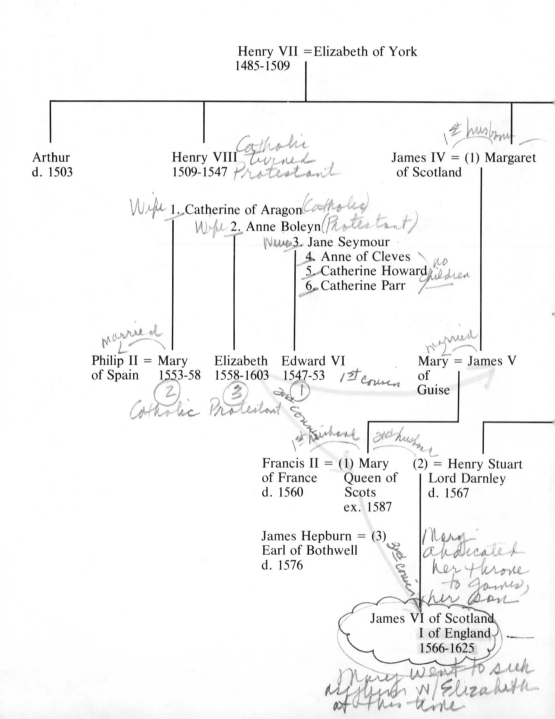

Henry VII = Elizabeth of York
1485-1509

Arthur
d. 1503

Henry VIII *Catholic turned Protestant*
1509-1547

James IV = (1) Margaret
of Scotland   *1st husband*

Wife 1. Catherine of Aragon *(Catholic)*
Wife 2. Anne Boleyn *(Protestant)*
None 3. Jane Seymour
4. Anne of Cleves
5. Catherine Howard   *no children*
6. Catherine Parr

Married
Philip II = Mary
of Spain   1553-58
②

Elizabeth
1558-1603
③

Edward VI
1547-53
①

1st cousin

Catholic Protestant *3rd cousin*

married
Mary = James V
of
Guise

1st husband   *3rd husband*

Francis II = (1) Mary
of France   Queen of
d. 1560   Scots
             ex. 1587

(2) = Henry Stuart
     Lord Darnley
     d. 1567

James Hepburn = (3)
Earl of Bothwell
d. 1576

3rd cousin

Mary abdicated her throne to James, her son

James VI of Scotland
I of England
1566-1625

Mary went to such lengths w/ Elizabeth at this time

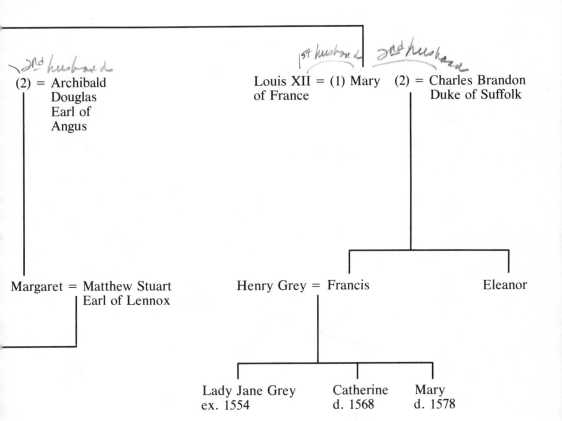

(2) = Archibald
    Douglas
    Earl of
    Angus

Louis XII = (1) Mary (2) = Charles Brandon
of France   Duke of Suffolk

Margaret = Matthew Stuart   Henry Grey = Francis   Eleanor
        Earl of Lennox

Lady Jane Grey   Catherine   Mary
ex. 1554   d. 1568   d. 1578

I. THE CONTEMPORARIES SPEAK

Sir John Hayward

ANNALS

John Hayward (1564-1627) was a successful lawyer and somewhat less successful historian who had to await the succession of James I for full recognition of his loyalty and talents. He wrote two books in support of James's favorite subjects—the divine right of kings and the union of England and Scotland—and was knighted in 1619. The honor had in part been denied him by Elizabeth because Hayward angered the Queen by the publication of his first book in 1599, which dealt with the overthrow of Richard II and the triumph of Henry IV. It was a subject guaranteed to alarm the Queen, who was particularly touchy about successful usurpers because of her troubles with the Earl of Essex. To make matters worse, Hayward dedicated his history to the Earl, which so antagonized Elizabeth that she suggested that Hayward had merely lent his name to the volume and someone higher up had actually written it. She urged that the author be tortured in order to reveal the truth, but Francis Bacon dissuaded her, noting that it was always dangerous to rack a scholar and that she should content herself instead with tearing apart his style. Hayward spent at least a year in prison for his poor sense of timing, if not for any proven treason. His *Annals of the First Four Years of the Reign of Queen Elizabeth,* from which the following selection comes, was written long after his release, possibly during the 1610s, but it was not published until 1840. Despite Elizabeth's severe treatment of Hayward, the *Annals* depict Gloriana on the day of her coronation in a remarkably favorable light.

UPON THE fourteenth day of January [1559], in the afternoon, she passed from the Tower through the City of London to Westminster, most royally furnished, both for her person and for her train, knowing right well that in pompous ceremonies a secret of government doth much consist, for that the people are naturally both taken and held with exterior shows. The nobility and gentlemen were very many, and no less honorably furnished. The rich attire, the ornaments, the beauty of ladies, did add particular graces to the solemnity, and held the eyes and hearts of men dazzled between contentment and admiration. When she took her coach within the Tower, she made a solemn thanksgiving to God, that He had delivered her no less mercifully, no less mightily from her im-

From Sir John Hayward, *Annals of the First Four Years of the Reign of Queen Elizabeth,* ed. John Bruce (London: Camden Society, 1840), pp. 15–18.

prisonment in that place, than He had delivered Daniel from the lions' den: that He preserved her from those dangers wherewith she was both environed and overwhelmed, to bring her to the joy and honor of that day. As she passed through the City, nothing was omitted to do her the highest honors, which the citizens (who could procure good use both of purses and inventions) were able to perform. It were the part of an idle orator to describe the pageants, the arches, and other well devised honors done unto her; the order, the beauty, the majesty of this action, the high joy of some, the silence and reverence of others, the constant contentment of all; their untired patience never spent, either with long expecting (some of them from a good part of the night before) or with insatiable beholding the ceremonies of that day.

The Queen was not negligent on her part to descend to all pleasing behavior, which seemed to proceed from a natural gentleness of disposition, and not from any strained desire of popularity or insinuation. She gave due respect to all sorts of persons, wherein the quickness of her spirit did work more actively than did her eyes. When the people made the air ring with praying to God for her prosperity, she thanked them with exceeding liveliness both of countenance and voice, and wished neither prosperity nor safety to herself, which might not be for their common good. As she passed by the Companies of the City, standing in their liveries, she took particular knowledge of them, and graced them with many witty formalities of speech. She diligently both observed and commended such devices as were presented unto her, and to that end sometimes caused her coach to stand still, sometimes to be removed to places of best advantage for hearing and for sight; and in the meantime fairly entreated the people to be silent. And when she understood not the meaning of any representation, or could not perfectly hear some speeches that were made, she caused the same to be declared unto her.

When the Recorder of the City presented to her a purse of crimson satin, very richly and curiously wrought, and therein a thousand marks in gold, with request that she would continue a gracious mistress to the City, she answered that she was bound in natural obligations so to do, not so much for their gold as for their good wills; that as they had been at great expense of treasure that day to honor her passage, so all the days of her life she would be ready to expend not only her treasure but the dearest drops of her blood to maintain and increase their flourishing estate. When she spied a pageant at the Little Conduite in Cheape, she demanded (as it was her custom in the rest) what should be represented therein. Answer was made that Time did there attend for her. "Time?" said she. "How is that possible, seeing it is time that hath brought me hither?" Here a Bible in English, richly covered, was let down unto her by a silk lace from a child that represented truth. She kissed both her hands, with both her hands she received it, then she kissed it; afterwards applied it to her breast; and lastly held it up, thanking the City especially for that gift, and promising to be a diligent reader thereof. When any good wishes were cast forth for her virtuous and religious government, she would lift up her hands toward heaven, and desire the people to answer "Amen." When it was told her that an ancient citizen turned his head back and wept, [she said,] "I warrant you...it is for joy"; and so in very deed it was. She cheerfully received not only rich gifts from persons of worth, but nosegays, flowers, rosemary branches, and such like presents, offered unto her from very mean persons, insomuch as it may truly be said, that there was neither courtesy nor cost cast away that day upon her. It is incredible how often she caused her coach to stay, when any made offer to approach unto her, whether to make petition or whether to manifest their loving affections.

Hereby the people, to whom no music

is so sweet as the affability of their prince, were so strongly stirred to love and joy that all men contended how they might more effectually testify the same; some with plausible acclamations, some with sober prayers, and many with silent and true-hearted tears, which were then seen to melt from their eyes. and afterwards, departing home, they so stretched everything to the highest strain, that they inflamed the like affections in others. It is certain that these high humilities, joined to justice, are of greater power to win the hearts of people than any, than all other virtues beside. All other virtues are expedient for a prince, all are advised, but these are necessary, these are enjoined; without many others a prince may stand, but without these upon every occasion he stands in danger.

The day following, being Sunday, she was, with all accustomed ceremonies, crowned in the Abbey Church at Westminster; having made demonstration of so many princely virtues before, that all men were of opinion that one crown was not sufficient to adorn them.

Count de Feria

LETTER TO THE KING OF SPAIN

Gomez Suarez de Figueroa of Cordova, Count de Feria (died 1571) accompanied Philip II of Spain to England, where he met his future wife, Jane Dormer, lady-in-waiting to Queen Mary. Later he was sent by Philip as ambassador to help handle the difficult transition from Mary to Elizabeth and thereby to influence the new Queen. In this he signally failed, and quickly Elizabeth and the Count developed an intense dislike for one another. His report on the new sovereign (December 14, 1558) was written less than a month after her succession, a month before her coronation, and a fortnight before his own marriage to Jane. He left England with his bride in May of 1559 and spent the rest of his life as a grandee living on his estates. He was created duke in 1567, and just before his death he was appointed governor of the Spanish Low Countries. Feria's attitude toward Elizabeth was predictable: as a man, as a Spaniard, and as a Catholic he expected nothing but trouble from Anne Boleyn's daughter on the English throne.

IT GIVES ME great trouble every time I write to your Majesty not to be able to send more pleasing intelligence, but what can be expected from a country governed by a Queen, and she is a young lass who, although sharp, is without prudence, and is every day standing up against religion more openly? The kingdom is entirely in the hands of young folks, heretics and traitors, and the Queen does not favor a single man whom Her Majesty, who is now in heaven, [the

From Count de Feria, "Letter to the King of Spain, 14 December 1558," in *Calendar of Letters and State Papers relating to English Affairs in the Archives of Simancas,* ed. M.A.S. Hume (London, 1892), I, No. 4, p. 7.

late Queen Mary] would have received and will take no one into her service who served her sister when she was Lady Mary. On her way from the tower to her house where she now is, she saw the Marquis of Northampton, who is ill with a quartan ague, at a window and she stopped her palfrey and was for a long while asking him about his health in the most cordial way in the world. The only true reason for this was that he had been a great traitor to her sister, and he who was most prominent in this way is now best thought of. The old people and the Catholics are dissatisfied, but dare not open their lips. She seems to me incomparably more feared than her sister and gives her orders and has her way as absolutely as her father did.

Guzman de Silva

LETTER TO THE KING OF SPAIN

Don Diego Guzman de Silva (died 1578) was a minor church official, a professional diplomat, and a civil servant. He was appointed resident ambassador to England by Philip II of Spain in June of 1564 and remained in England four years. His description of Elizabeth, whom he admired but did not approve, was written shortly before his departure from London in September of 1568.

THE QUEEN arrived in this city [London] on the 6th in good health and continued her progress which, as I have said, will only be in the neighborhood, as she is careful to keep near at hand when troubles and disturbances exist in adjacent countries. She came by the river as far as Reading, and thence through the country in a carriage, open on all sides, that she might be seen by the people who flocked all along the roads as far as the Duke of Norfolk's houses where she alighted. She was received everywhere with great acclamations and signs of joy, as is customary in this country; whereat she was extremely pleased and told me so, giving me to understand how beloved she was by her subjects and how highly she esteemed this, together with the fact they were peaceful and contented whilst her neighbors on all sides are in such trouble. She attributed it all to God's miraculous goodness. She ordered her carriage to be taken sometimes where the crowd seemed thickest and stood up and thanked the people.

From Guzman de Silva, ''Letter to the King of Spain,'' in *Calendar of Letters and State Papers relating to English Affairs in the Archives of Simancas,* ed. M.A.S. Hume (London, 1894), II, No. 37, pp. 50-51.

Lupold von Wedel

A KNIGHT ERRANT

Lupold von Wedel of Kremzow (1544-1615) was a perambulatory German aristocrat who for almost thirty years of his life roamed the length and breadth of Europe and the Near East as a traveler and professional soldier. He spent seven years fighting the Turks, traveled to Cairo and Jerusalem, visited every major city in Italy and Germany, fought in the French wars of religion, and took a short "tour" of England and Scotland between August of 1584 and April of 1585. Being a Protestant, Wedel tended to look upon Elizabeth as a heroine, the defender of the true faith against the Antichrist of Catholicism and the aggression of Spain.

O N THE 27th December which was the third and last day of holy Christmastide, I went five miles down the Thames to Grunewitz [Greenwich], where the Queen is now in residence. Arrived at the palace, I first went into the chapel which is hung with gold. The pulpit is covered with red gold-embroidered velvet. In one half of the church stands a large, high, gilded altar and there, divided off from the rest, is a recess entirely of gold cloth out of which the Queen comes when she is about to receive the Sacrament. Then I went into a large roon before the Queen's chamber hung with tapestry wrought in silver and gold. Here I waited until she went to church....She was accompanied to church by her gentlemen and ladies-in-waiting, who, however, on this occasion, it being Christmastide, were more gorgeously dressed. But the Queen being in mourning for the Duc d'Alencon [died 1584] and the Prince of Orange [murdered 1584], was dressed in black velvet sumptuously embroidered with

silver and pearls. Over her robe she had a silver shawl, that was full of meshes and diaphanous like a piece of gossamer tissue. But this shawl gleamed as though it were bespangled with tinsel, which, however, was not the case, and it hung down over her robe as low as the hem of her skirt. While she was at church a long table was made ready in the room previously described, under the canopy of cloth of gold. On her return from church there were served at this table forty large and silver dishes, all of gilt silver, with various meats. She alone took her seat at the table. At no other time throughout the whole year does the Queen dine in public, and it is only on feast days that a stranger can see her at meals. After the Queen had sat down, a table was set up at the end of the room near the door, and at this table five countesses took their seats. A young gentleman habited in black carved the meats for the Queen, and a gentleman of about the same age arrayed in green, served her beverages. This gentleman had to remain kneeling as

From Lupold von Wedel, "A Knight Errant," in *Queen Elizabeth and Some Foreigners*, ed. Victor von Klarwell, trans. T.H. Nash (New York: Brentano's, 1928), pp. 335-338. Reprinted by permission of the publisher.

long as she was drinking; when she had finished, he rose and removed the goblet. At the table, to her right, stood gentlemen of rank, as for instance my Lord Hower [Charles Howard, later Earl of Nottingham]. He is styled Chamberlain, but has the rank of a Lord High Steward in Germany. There stood further Mylord Lester, the Master of the Horse [Robert Dudley, Earl of Leicester]. He is said to have had a love-affair with the Queen for a long time. Now he has a wife. Then there was the Lord High Treasurer and the Keeper of the Privy Purse Mylord Hertford [Edward Seymour], who, they say, of all Englishmen has the most right to the Throne. He it is who got one of the Queen's ladies with child and married another much against the Queen's will. Therefore he fell into disgrace, but is now again restored to favour. Further there was Christopher Hatten [Hatton], Captain of the Bodyguard, who is said to have been her lover after Lester. All of them had white staffs in their hands and were handsome old gentlemen. If she summoned one of them, as often happened—for, as a rule, she speaks continuously—he had to kneel until she commanded him to rise. Then they made her a low bow and retired. When they came to the centre of the room they again bowed, stepped down from the dais and had the next course served up. They walked before the bearers of the viands [meats], who were knights and nobles. Of the dishes there were now only twenty-four. In the room they had to bow three times with the food. They had previously done the same with the serviettes and all the table-ware, although the Queen was not yet present in the room. Four gentlemen with the sceptres that are carried before the Queen also walked before the dish bearers. On either side of the room, but not near the table, there stood as long as the meal lasted, knights, squires and ladies near those who were in charge of the magnificent drinking vessels. Her musicians were also in the apartment and discoursed excellent music. When the first dishes had been removed and others placed upon the table, she did not continue dining much longer, but soon rose from table. Just before she did so the five aforesaid countesses rose from their table and having twice made a deep courtesy to the Queen, passed over to the other side. Then the Queen rose and turned her back upon the table, whereupon two biships stepped forward and said grace. After them came three earls, one of whom was the son of the beheaded Duke of Nortfech [Norfolk].... These three then took a large basin, which was covered like a meat-dish and of gilt silver, and two of the old gentlemen held the towel. The five of them then advanced to the Queen and knelt down before her. They then raised the lid from the basin which was held by two of them. A third poured water over the Queen's hands, who before washing her hands drew off a ring and handed it to the above-named Lord Chamberlain. After washing her hands she again drew on the ring. She then took an Earl's son by his cloak and retired with him to a bow-window. He knelt down before her and had a long talk. When he had gone she seated herself on the floor on a cushion, summoned a young gentleman who likewise knelt before her and conversed. On his leaving she called a countess who, like the gentleman, knelt before her.

Cardinal William Allen

ADMONITION TO THE NOBILITY AND PEOPLE OF ENGLAND

Cardinal William Allen (1532-1594) was born in Lancashire. He was forced to flee England in 1561 as a consequence of his efforts to proselytize his faith and convert Englishmen to Catholicism. He established the English (Catholic) College at Douai to train seminary priests who returned in secret to England to continue the work of conversion. Upon being created a Cardinal in 1587, Allen wrote the following open "letter" to his countrymen, twenty thousand copies of which supposedly were printed in anticipation of the triumph of the Spanish Armada. How many copies of the *Admonition to the Nobility and People of England and Ireland concerning the Present Warres made for the execution of his Holines Sentence, by the highe and mightie Kinge Catholike of Spaine* actually accompanied the Spanish fleet or found their way into the homes of English Catholics is unknown, but the "letter" is a good example of sixteenth-century religious writing, and it is an important corrective to the picture of the Queen produced by her admirers. Simply in terms of head count, there were many more Europeans who saw Elizabeth as the disciple of the devil rather than as the heroine of her age.

BRIEFLY and plainly we will set down what manner of woman she is against whom this holy enterprise [Armada] is made; how she intruded into that dignity wherein she standeth; how she has behaved herself both at home and abroad; by what laws of God and man her punishment is pursued,...seeing it proceedeth from so lawful authority, so just grounds, so holy intentions, and tendeth to so happy an end, and is to be executed by so sure and sweet means, and chosen persons.

And first of all it is notorious to the whole world that Henry [VIII], the supposed father to this pretended Queen...was in sin for his horrible sacrilegious murdering of saints and rebellion against God's Church. He was lawfully excommunicated and deprived by Paul III in the year 1535, and therewithal by name and in particular all the issue that should proceed of his incestuous copulation with Anne Boleyn was most justly declared illegitimate and incapable of succession to the crown of England. Also by the sentence of said Paul, and his predecessor Clement the VIIth in the year of our Lord 1533 (both which stand in their full force still), as by sundry acts of Parliament made by Henry himself and never repealed, legitimizing her sister and declaring her to be base, she must needs be adjudged by law and nature unable to inherit the crown....

From Cardinal William Allen, *An Admonition to the Nobility and People of England and Ireland concerning the Present Warres made for the Execution of his Holines Sentence, by the highe and mightie Kinge Catholike of Spaine* (Antwerp, 1588), pp. VIII–XXIX. The selection has been heavily edited; the spelling, punctuation and word usage modernized to make the passage intelligible to the modern reader.

But howsoever she be descended or possessed of the crown, her manifold wickedness is so heinous and intolerable that for the same she has been in person justly deposed by the sentences of three sundry popes, whereunto if we add the two former censures condemning her incestuous nativity and generation, we shall find that she hath been condemned by five declaratory judicial sentences of God's Church.

And to begin with the highest and most heinous crime of all against God and His Church, she is convicted of many damnable heresies and open rebellion against God's Church and See Apostolic, for which she is so notoriously known, termed and taken for an heretic, as well at home as abroad, that she provided by a special act of Parliament that none should call her heretic, schismatic, tyrant, usurper or infidel, under pain of high treason.

She usurped by Luciferian pride the title of Supreme Ecclesiastical Governor, a thing in a woman, in all men's memory, unheard of nor tolerable to the masters of her own sect, and to Catholics in the world most ridiculous, absurd and detestable....

She unlawfully intruded herself, as before I have said, into possession of the crown of England...by enforced unjust laws, partly made by her supposed father being then an excommunicated person, and partly enacted by herself and her accomplices in the beginning of her pretended reign, being indeed taken and known for an incestuous bastard, begotten and born in sin, of an infamous courtesan Anne Boleyn, afterward executed for adultery, heresy and incest, amongst others with her natural brother....

She is guilty of perjury and high impiety for that she did break, violate and deride the solemn oath and promise made in her coronation to defend the ecclesiastical liberties and privileges granted by the ancient Christian kings of our realm, and by her contempt of the holy ceremony used in the anointing and investing of all faithful princes, wherein her wickedness was so notorious that the principal prelate to whom by ancient order...that function appertained, dared not, for fear of God and respect of his conscience, anoint her.

She did immediately upon her said intrusion, violently against all law and order, to the perdition of infinite souls, abolish the whole Catholic religion and faith, that all the former faithful kings of our country honorably lived and died in; repealing at the same time all the godly acts that Queen Mary, the only lawful daughter of King Henry VIII, made for the reconciliation of the realm to the unity of God's universal Church again; and she revived all the impious statutes made by her foresaid supposed father and brother [Edward VI] against God, the Church and the See Apostolic. She severed herself and subjects violently from the society of all Catholic countries and from the fellowship of all faithful princes and priests in the world.

She did at the same time abolish or profane all the holy sacraments of Christ's Church, particularly the very blessed and sovereign sacrifice of Christ's body and blood, erecting for the same high idolatry and polluted bread of schism and abominable desolation.

She did shut up both pulpits and churches from all Catholic priests, preachers and people. She caused all God's public,...constraining by great penalties and extreme punishment many thousand poor Christian souls of every degree and sex, to forsake their faith and religion, in which they and all their forefathers were baptized and brought up, ever since the realm was first converted to Christ, to the great torment of their minds and consciences and shortening of their days.

She impiously despoiled all sanctified places, [removing] their holy images, relics, memories and monuments of Christ our Savior, and of his blessed mother and saints; her own detestable cognizance [coat of arms] and other profane portraitures and paintings were exalted in their places; and she overthrew, destroyed and robbed all holy altars, chalices, vestments, church books and sacred vessels....

She hath seized upon the sacred persons of God's anointed, even of very bishops that had charge of her soul, called them to account for their preachings and doctrine, convented [summoned] them before her profane councillors and commissioners, deposed and imprisoned them with all others that were of learning and dignity among the clergy, until by the misery of their captivity they be in effect wholly worn and wasted away.

She hath caused the priests of God violently to be plucked from the altar... and to be carried in scornful manner revested [dressed in ecclesiastical regalia] through the streets, and exposed to all the ungodly villainy, derision [mockery], fury and folly of the simple and barbarous people: a thing certain that above all other kinds of irreligiousity most deserveth and soonest procureth God's vengeance.

She hath suppressed all the religious houses of both sexes, so many as were restored after her father's former horrible spoil, dispersed the professed of the same, and robbed them of all their lands and possessions.

She hath by unjust tyrannical statutes injuriously invaded the lands and goods of Catholic nobles and gentlemen...and she hath molested, disgraced, imprisoned and despoiled many at home of all degrees because they would not give oath and agreement to her anti-Christian and unnatural proud challenge of supremacy, nor honor her profane communion board. As a result, some provinces be in manner wholly bereaved of their just gentlemen in administration of the laws, and the people exceedingly annoyed by the loss of so good lords and so greathouse keepers, for lack of whom the poor daily perish.

Besides all which sacrilegious abominations and extortions against God, His Church and her own people, she hath endangered the kingdom and country by this great alteration of religion, which thing is never without inevitable peril, or sure ruin of the commonwealth. [She has also ruined the commonwealth] by great contempt and abasing of the ancient nobility; repealing them from due government, offices and places of honor; thrusting them to shameful and odious offices of inquisition upon Catholic men, to the great vexation and terror of their own consciences; forcing them through fear and desire of her favor, and of her base leaders', to condemn that in others which in their hearts and consciences they believe; and putting into their houses and chambers, traitors, spies, delators [informers] and promoters that take watch for her of all their ways, words and writings. The majority be already ruined most lamentably, and the rest stand in continual thralldom, danger and dishonor. So jealous be all tyrants and usurpers of their state, and so loath they are to be seconded by any other than of their own creation!

She hath to the shame and despite [scorn] [of the nobility], advanced base and unpure persons, inflamed with infinite avarice and ambition, men of great partiality, bribery and iniquity, to the highest honors and most profitable offices of her court and country, repelling from all public action, charge and authority, under color of religion, the wisest, godliest, learnedest and sincerest of all sorts of men, to the special annoyance and dishonor of the whole state....

She hath laid the country wide open to be a place of refuge and sanctuary of all athiests, Anabaptists, heretics and rebels of all nations, and replenished sundry the coast towns and others with innumerable strangers of the worst sort of malefactors and sectaries, to the great impoverishing of the inhabitants and no small peril of the whole realm. The number and quality of [these strangers] is such that when time may serve and favor them, they may give a sturdy battle to the inhabitants of the realm.

She hath not spared to oppress her subjects (never having just wars with any king or country in the world) with manifold exactions not only by ordinary means of more frequent and larger subsidies [parliamentary taxes] (for which only end she hath had more parliaments than ever any lawful prince had) but also by sundry shameful guiles of lotteries, laws, decrees and sales of money and such like deceits. She hath employed the riches of the realm to set up and sustain rebels and heretics against their natural princes, to the great dishonor of our nation, damage and danger of our merchants, as well of all other travelers. A public piracy and robbery both by sea and land has been authorized by her letters of marque, and she hath otherwise permitted divers wicked persons to despoil whom they like, making certain that some piece of the gain returns to some of her own chief councillors and officers.

She doth for money and bribes, to the enriching of herself and servants, by licenses, dispensations, pardons and permissions, abolish or frustrate many profitable laws; as she doth to the same end multiply sundry frivolous acts with great forfeits to the transgressors....By which wicked traffic and other pitiful pillage of the people, some of her creatures are grown so great and insolent that all estates and degrees within the realm stand in awe and danger of them.

In which sort, besides others whom we need not note, she hath exalted one special extortioner [Robert Dudley]...to serve her filthy lust, whereof to have the more freedom and interest, he (as many be presumed by her consent) caused his own wife cruelly to be murdered....[Now as her] amorous minion, he is advanced to high office, degree, and excessive wealth, and is become her chief leader in all her wicked and unwonted course of regiment. He is her instrument of destruction of the nobility by many indirect means, and of the ruining, abasing, disgracing, disauthorizing divers ancient houses, names and persons of renown.

Moreover, innumerable of the commonality perished most pitifully in sundry provinces for the feeding of his infinite avarice, and his insatiable companions and retainers live only of bribery, spoil and robbery: whereby, and through the favor of the pretended Queen, he hath this many a year overruled the chamber, court, council, parliament, ports, forts, seas, shops, borders, men, munitions, and all the country. He hath had still at his command all officers, justices, benches, bars and sessions; hath had the sale and monopoly of all laws, offices, licenses, forfeits, bishoprics, benefices and colleges; hath made such traffic...about the treasures, prerogatives, lands and commodities of the crown that he hath enabled and fortified himself far above the measure of any English subject, and hath been the principal disturber and destroyer of the provinces round about us, to the impoverishment of the people at home and decay of all traffic abroad, with extreme peril of the land.

With the foresaid person and divers others she hath abused her body, against God's laws, to the disgrace of princely majesty, and with the whole nation's reproach. By unspeakable and incredible variety of lust, which modesty suffereth not to be remembered...she hath defiled and infamed [dishonored] her person and country, and made her court as a trap, by this damnable and detestable art. By entangling in sin and overthrowing the younger sort of the nobility and gentlemen of the land, she is become notorious to the world, and in other countries a common fable for this her turpitude, which in so high degree, namely in a woman and a Queen, deserveth not only deposition but all vengeance both of God and man, and cannot be tolerated without the eternal infamy of our whole country. The whole world derides our effeminate dastardy that has suffered such a creature almost thirty years together to reign both over our bodies and souls, and to have the chief regiment of all our affairs as well spiritual as temporal, to the extinguishing not only of religion but of all chaste living and honesty....

Although the principal peers of the realm and others of high authority as deputies from the whole Parliament made humble suit and supplication to her that, for pity and compassion of their desolate case and because of the danger that the whole realm, especially the nobility, should be in if she deceased without lawful issue and with so many competitors for the crown, she should therefore marry and procure (if it were God's pleasure) lawful heirs of her body to inherit her dominions after her. Sometimes she merely and mockingly answered that she would die a maiden Queen, but afterwards in contempt and rebuke of all the estates of the realm, and to the condemnation of chaste and lawful marriage...she forced the very Parliament itself to give consent and to provide by a pretended law...that none should so much as be named for her successor during her life, saving a natural, that is to say bastard-born, child of her own body. A wonderful thralldom, a lamentable case, that this high court of old, so renowned for freedom and justice, should now be at the devotion of one woman so far as to authorize both her shameful incontinency and pernicious obstinacy against the honor and good of the whole realm, and with no cause in the world why the next lawful heir may not better bear the naming...saving that it might be prejudicial to her private and present peace, which she ever prefereth before the public!...Usurpers always stand in more awe of the next heir and successor than lawful princes commonly do.

She, all this not withstanding, in the mean season, as often before and after promised marriage to some of the nobility at home, making many of them stay single to the danger of their souls and decay of their families. She also deeply dallied and abused by dissembling almost all of the great personages of Europe, to whom, as well by letters as by solemn embassies, she proffered herself, to the mockery and final dilution [weakening] of them all, to her own infamy, and the danger of her people. Especially of late years she hath most pitifully and devilishly abused the late noble brother of France [the Duke of Anjou]. By manifold hope and promise of her marriage and crown...the poor young gentleman was driven into those dangerous actions and dishonorable affairs of heretics and rebels, to his great dishonor, and likely shortening of his days.

By all which dishonorable and unworthy dealings, the whole world may see that in atheism and epicurism she would...turn the like and whole weal of our country, once most flourishing, to the feeding of her own disordered delights, being loath no doubt that anything should be left after her life that her rage and riot had not overrun, or that her realm should be extant any longer than she might make pleasure of it. [Glad she may be] that so flourishing and ancient a commonwealth, which she hath in manner brought to destruction in her life, might be buried in her ignominious ashes when she is dead. Wherein her affection is so passing unnatural that she hath been heard to wish that the day after her death she might stand in some high place between heaven and earth to behold the scrambling that she conceived would be for the crown, enjoying herself in the conceit and foresight of our future miseries.... She is not unlike to Nero, who intending for his recreation to let Rome on fire, devised an eminent pillar whereon himself might stand to behold it....

Besides all these outrages in her person and regiment, and besides sundry wicked attempts and treasons before she came to the crown, she hath showed such faithless dealing toward all near neighbors—most just, mighty and Catholic kings abroad—that it is almost incredible. Some she hath ignominiously despoiled of great treasures; one [Mary Queen of Scots] that fled to her for promised succor and safety—yea, even her that was our true, lawful and worthy sovereign—she hath against all law of God, nature and nations, after long imprisonment, at length also murdered; and some she hath in great simulation of friendship in effect broken most ancient leagues and amity. Against them all, she hath not only notoriously confederated herself with their rebels, Huguenots, Guises, publicans [those excommunicated by the church] and malcontents, giving them men, munition and money, with much continual encouragement and counsel in all their wicked attempts, but also was and yet is known to be the first and principal fountain of all these furious rebellions in Scotland, France and Flanders, to the fall almost of all their whole states and the great calamity of the Church of God. It is evident to all the world that she reigneth unlawfully as a usurper and rebel, who only standeth and holdeth herself up all this while by joining with traitors and rebels, and succoring them against their lawful princes and sovereigns.

In this kind she hath by the execrable [detestable] practices of some of her chief ministers, as by their own hands, letters and instructions...it may be proved, sent abroad exceedingly great numbers of intelligencers, spies and practicers, into most princes' courts, cities and commonwealths in Christendom, not only to take and give secret notices of princes' intentions but also to deal with the discontented in every stage against their lords and superiors, namely against his Holiness and King of Spain, whose sacred persons they have fought many ways wickedly to destroy. Furthermore it is evident she hath by messengers and letters dealt with the cruel and dreadful tyrant and enemy of our faith—the Great Turk himself (against whom our noble kings have in old time so valiantly fought and vowed themselves to all perils and peregrinations)—for the invasion of some parts of Christendom....

By which Machiavellian, godless and conscienceless course, unjust usurped regiments [governments] be always conducted; advanced not by counsel or courage but by plain trumpery, treason and cosingage [cheating]; working their own peace, wealth and felicity by their neighbors' wars, woe, misery. This never endeth well nor endureth long, nor is in sin unrevenged, although the present prosperity, upholden by others' calamity, hath distracted the simple and worldly from the beholding of that extreme plague, which always both by God's justice and man's revenge ensueth of the same....

Besides all other insolences and glorious vanities and vaunts [braggings] in her words, cracks, countenances and gestures, in all her life and behavior (in which kind she exceedeth all creatures living), she hath caused the annual day of her coronation in all parts of the realm to be sacredly kept and solemnized with ringing, singing, shows and ceremonies, and far more vacation from all servile labors than any day either of our blessed lord or lady. And even more abominable, having abolished the solemn feast of our blessed lady's nativity, she hath caused her own impure birthday to be solemnly celebrated, and put into the calendar the very eve of the said holy feast, and she put out the name of another saint on the 17th of November to place the memory of her coronation....

Now of all these heinous horrible facts, not credible almost to be achieved by one woman...she hath in sin showed herself incorrigible and altogether impatient of admonition...and to show herself wholly sold to sin, she hath now eighteen years stood stubbornly, contemptuously and obdurately. As in the sight of God by her own willful separation through schism and heresy [she was] condemned before, so now by name [she is] notoriously excommunicated and deposed in the word of Christ and omnipotent power of God by sentence given against her by holy Pius V, the highest court of religion under the heavens. The which state of excommunication (though presently of the faithless, where there is no sense of religion, it be not felt nor feared) is most miserable, most horrible, and most near to damnation of all things that may happen to a man in this life: far more grievous (sayeth a certain glorious Doctor) than to be hewn in pieces with a sword, consumed by fire or devoured of wild beasts....

And she hath not only continued in this damnable contempt of the holy Church's censures so long as we have said, but also commanded and caused [the execution of] the publishers, defenders and approvers [of the church]...some being apprehended at home, and others traitorously bought and sold abroad and sent home, and all in cruel manner murdered —yea, and for their parts very willingly martyred to their eternal estimation, rather than they would live and serve any such heretic, atheist and usurper....

Her obstinacy and Satanical obduration daily increasing, she hath these late years imbrued her hands and country with the sacred blood of a number of most innocent, learned and famous religious men, yea and holy bishops also in England and Ireland, causing them pitifully to be racked, rent, chained, famished, beaten, buffeted, derided, abused, and by false accusation of crimes never intended, under pretense of treason against her usurped state and person, to be finally with all cruelty executed to the regret and shame of our nation and wonder of all the world. And finally to accomplish the measure of all her inhumane cruelty, she hath this last year barbarously, unnaturally against the law of nations, by a statute of riot and conspiracy, murdered the Lady Mary of famous memory, Queen of Scotland, Dowager of France, God's anointed, her next kinswoman, and by law and right the true owner of the crown of England.

All which her open enormities, and other her secret wickedness hidden from us...may put all faithful and reasonable men out of doubt of the justice of the Apostolic sentence and censure against her, being well assured that if any case may fall, in which a prince may justly be forsaken or resisted by his subjects, or if any crime in the world either in life, regiment or religion can deserve deposition of a king, that here all causes together do concur in the person of the pretended queen in the highest degree.

André Hurault, Sieur de Maisse

SELECTIONS FROM *A JOURNAL*

André Hurault was charged by Henry IV of France with the delicate mission of discovering whether Elizabeth was willing to join France in peace negotiations with Spain or whether she preferred to continue the war, and if so, on what conditions. The implied threat, of course, was that Elizabeth might have to fight the war alone.

From Sieur de Maisse, *A Journal of All That Was Accomplished by Monsieur de Maisse, Ambassador in England from King Henri IV to Queen Elizabeth, Anno Domini 1597,* trans. and ed. G.B. Harrison (London: The Nonesuch Press, 1931), pp. 3, 11-12, 14, 22-26, 36-39, 55-61, 94-95, 104, 108-111. Reprinted by permission of the author.

Although Henry was bound by treaty not to make peace without England, both sovereigns knew this would not stop France if it were to her self-interest to end the war. Hurault arrived in England on November 30, 1597 and departed January 17, 1598. His *Journal* is primarily the record of his diplomatic discussions with the Queen, but is also interspersed with lighter, more intimate touches, as the following extracts reveal.

I REACHED London in the evening of this second day of the month of December, night having fallen, and was lodged in a house that the Queen had commanded for me wherein Drake had formerly lodged. What I learned of the Queen and of the principal of her Council before I had seen either her or any of them is that when a man speaks to her, and especially when he says something displeasing, she interrupts not seldom; and by reason of her interruptions very often she misunderstands what is said to her and misreports it to her Council. Hence comes the custom of delivering to the Council in writing what has been said to her. She is a haughty woman, falling easily into rebuke, and above all when any speak on behalf of the King [of France], whom she considers for a long time to have been greatly beholding to her. In her own nature she is very avaricious, and when some expense is necessary her Councillors must deceive her before embarking her on it little by little. She thinks highly of herself and has little regard for her servants and Council, being of opinion that she is far wiser than they; she mocks them and often cries out upon them. On their part they...have given her a high opinion of her wisdom and prudence. She thinks also that this is due to her age, saying quite freely that she was intended for affairs of state, even from her cradle; she told me so herself....

Her government is fairly pleasing to the people, who show that they love her, but it is little pleasing to the great men and the nobles; and if by chance she should die, it is certain that the English would never again submit to the rule of a woman....

When she moves into the country, it is ordinarily at the expense of those with whom she lodges; and even then at her departure must they give her presents, a custom that has been introduced in her time by the Earl of Leicester, and maintained to such a degree that there is now no one at Court but gives her the like at certain feasts, as on her birthday, her coronation day, and on such occasions; and when they cannot give her anything else, she gladly takes a dozen angels [gold coins each worth about 8 shillings]. They say that not a year passes but the Earl of Essex gives her 10,000 or 12,000 crowns....

On the 8th of December I did not think to be given an audience for that day and was resolved to make my complaint; but about one hour after noon there came a gentleman from the Queen who said to me that her Majesty was much grieved that she had not given me audience sooner, and that she prayed me to come to her that very hour. He brought me in a coach to take me down to the river where one of the barges awaited me, and we went thence to the gate of the Queen's palace. At our landing there came to seek me a gentleman who spoke very good Italian, called Monsieur Wotton, who told me that her Majesty sent word that I should be very welcome and that she was awaiting me....

He led me across a chamber of moderate size wherein were the guards of the Queen, and thence into the Presence Chamber, as they call it, in which all present, even though the Queen be absent, remain uncovered. He then conducted me to a place on one side, where there was a cushion made ready for me. I waited there some time, and the Lord Chamberlain, who has the charge of the Queen's household (not as *maître d'hôtel,* but to arrange audiences and to escort those who demand them and especially ambassadors), came to seek me where I was seated. He led me along a passage somewhat dark, into a chamber that they call the Privy Chamber, at the head of which was the Queen seated in a low chair, by herself, and withdrawn from all the lords and ladies that were present, they being in one place and she in another. After I had made her my reverence at the entry of the chamber, she rose and came five or six paces towards me, almost into the middle of the chamber. I kissed the fringe of her robe and she embraced me with both hands. She looked at me kindly, and began to excuse herself that she had not sooner given me audience, saying that the day before she had been very ill with a gathering on the right side of her face, which I should never have thought seeing her eyes and face: but she did not remember ever to have been so ill before. She excused herself because I found her attired in her nightgown, and began to rebuke those of her Council who were present, saying, "What will these gentlemen say"—speaking of those who accompanied me—"to see me so attired? I am much disturbed that they should see me in this state."

Then I answered her that there was no need to make excuse on my account, for that I had come to do her service and honor, and not to give her inconvenience. She replied that I gave her none, and that she saw me willingly. I told her that the King had commanded me to visit her and to kiss her hands on his behalf, and charged me to learn the news of her well-being and health, which (thanks be to God) I saw to be such as her servants and friends would desire; and which I

prayed God might continue for long years, and in all prosperity and dignity. She stood up while I was speaking, but then she returned to her chair when she saw that I was only speaking of general matters. I drew nearer to her chair and began to deal with her in that wherewithal I had been charged; and because I was uncovered, from time to time she signed to me with her hand to be covered, which I did. Soon after she caused a stool to be brought, whereon I sat and began to talk to her.

She was strangely attired in a dress of silver cloth, white and crimson, or silver "gauze," as they call it. This dress had slashed sleeves lined with red taffeta, and was girt about with other little sleeves that hung down to the crown, which she was for ever twisting and untying. She kept the front of her dress open, and one could see the whole of her bosom, and passing low, and often she would open the front of this robe with her hands as if she was too hot. The collar of the robe was very high, and the lining of the inner part all adorned with little pendants of rubies and pearls, very many, but quite small. She had also a chain of rubies and pearls about her neck. On her head she wore a garland of the same material and beneath it a great reddish-colored wig, with a great number of spangles of gold and silver, and hanging down over her forehead some pearls, but of no great worth. On either side of her ears hung two great curls of hair, almost down to her shoulders and within the collar of her robe, spangled as the top of her head. Her bosom is somewhat wrinkled as well as [one can see for] the collar that she wears round her neck, but lower down her flesh is exceeding white and delicate, so far as one could see.

As for her face, it is and appears to be very aged. It is long and thin, and her teeth are very yellow and unequal, compared with what they were formerly, so they say, and on the left side less than on the right. Many of them are missing so that one cannot understand her easily when she speaks quickly. Her figure is fair and tall and graceful in whatever she does; so far as may be she keeps her dignity, yet humbly and graciously withal.

All the time she spoke she would often rise from her chair, and appear to be very impatient with what I was saying. She would complain that the fire was hurting her eyes, though there was a great screen before it and she six or seven feet away; yet did she give orders to have it extinguished, making them bring water to pour upon it. She told me that she was well pleased to stand up, and that she used to speak thus with the ambassadors who came to seek her, and used sometimes to tire them, of which they would on occasion complain. I begged her not to overtire herself in any way, and I rose when she did; and then she sat down again, and so did I. At my departure she rose and conducted me to that same place where she had come to receive me, and again began to say that she was grieved that all the gentlemen I had brought should see her in that condition, and she called to see them. They made their reverence before her, one after the other, and she embraced them all with great charm and smiling countenance....

15th December. I thought that I should have appeared before the Queen. She was on point of giving me audience, having already sent her coaches to fetch me, but taking a look into her mirror said that she appeared too ill and that she was unwilling for anyone to see her in that state; and so countermanded me.

Today she sent her coaches and one of her own gentlemen servants to conduct me. When I alighted from my coach Monsieur de Mildmay, formerly ambassador in France, came up to me and led me to the Presence Chamber, where the Lord Chamberlain came to seek me as before and conducted me to the Privy Chamber where the Queen was standing by a window. She looked in better health than before. She was clad in a dress of black taffeta, bound with gold lace, and

like a robe in the Italian fashion with open sleeves and lined with crimson taffeta. She had a petticoat of white damask, girdled, and open in front, as was also her chemise, in such a manner that she often opened this dress and one could see all her belly, and even to her navel. Her head tire was the same as before. She had bracelets of pearl on her hands, six or seven rows of them. On her head tire she wore a coronet of pearls, of which five or six were marvellously fair. When she raises her head she has a trick of putting both hands on her gown and opening it insomuch that all her belly can be seen. She greeted me with very good cheer and embraced me, and then, having been some three feet from the window, she went and sat down on her chair of state and caused another to be brought to me, taking care to make me cover, which I did....

She often called herself foolish and old, saying she was sorry to see me there, and that, after having seen so many wise men and great princes, I should at length come to see a poor woman and a foolish. I was not without an answer, telling her the blessings, virtues and perfections that I had heard of her from stranger Princes, but that was nothing compared with what I saw. With that she was well contented, as she is when anyone commends her for her judgment and prudence, and she is very glad to speak slightingly of her intelligence and sway of mind, so that she may give occasion to commend her. She said that it was but natural that she should have some knowledge of the affairs of the world, being called thereto so young, and having worn that crown these forty years; but she said, and repeated often, that it came from the goodness of God, to which she was more beholding than anyone in the world. Thereupon she related to me the attempts that had been made as much against her life as against her state, holding it marvellous strange that the King of Spain should treat her in a fashion that she would never have believed to proceed from the will of a Prince; yet he had caused fifteen persons to be sent to that end, who had all confessed....When anyone speaks of her beauty she says that she was never beautiful, although she had that reputation thirty years ago. Nevertheless she speaks of her beauty as often as she can. As for her natural form and proportion, she is very beautiful; and by chance approaching a door and wishing to raise the tapestry that hung before it, she said to me laughing that she was as big as a door, meaning that she was tall.

It is certain that she was very greatly displeased that the King was unwilling to come and see her as he had promised, for she greatly desired these favours, and for it to be said that great princes have come to see her. During the siege of Rouen, thinking that the King was to come and see her, she went to Portsmouth with a great train, and she appeared to be vexed and to scoff that the King had not come thither....

The same day (24th December) I went to see the Queen, and she sent me her coaches. I found her very well and kindly disposed. She was having the spinet played to her in her chamber, seeming very attentive to it; and because I surprised her, or at least she feigned surprise, I apologised to her for diverting her from her pleasure. She told me that she loved music greatly and that she was having a pavanne [music for a sixteenth-century stately dance] played. I answered that she was a very good judge, and had the reputation of being a mistress in the art. She told me that she had meddled with it divers times, and still took great pleasure in it. She was clad in a white robe of cloth of silver, cut very low and her bosom uncovered. She had the same customary head attire, but diversified by several kinds of precious stones, yet not of any great value. She had a little gown of cloth of silver of peach colour, covered and hidden, which was fair.

My audience was long, during which she told me many tales of all kinds...She spoke to me at length of the things that they had said about her and made current in Rome, and that it was nothing but malice and lying. Amongst other things she said that Cardinal Cosmo had sent one of his own servants to London under the disguise of a merchant, who, addressing himself to an Italian, prayed him to conduct him to the place where they make the bears fight: "But," quoth he, "I am not content to see them. I would touch them." Then he confessed to this Italian that he had been sent here for that very reason because that the Queen was said to have caused the Catholics to be covered with bear skins and set to be eaten by dogs, and that it had been so reported in Rome. She told me also how it had been reported there that she caused a hundred and four Catholic women to die in one house; yet there never entered into this house more than one or two women; and these were lies that they told of her by malevolence. God is witness to her conscience that she has never allowed ill to be done to any Catholic for faith in his religion, save when they made attempt upon her state. She wished they could see the inside of her heart in a picture and that it was at Rome, so that all could see it as it was. We entered into talk about Pope Sixtus, and she told me how he had said to two of her gentlemen being in Rome that if this lady had not been a heretic she would have been the most perfect and accomplished Princess in the world, and but for that he would honour and serve her very willingly as more worthy of service than all the Princes of Christendom.

Thereupon she told me that if there were two Princes in Christendom who had good will and courage it would be easy to reconcile the differences in religion; for there was only one Jesus Christ and one faith, and all the rest that they disputed about but trifles. Then she ended by saying that she would not have either her body or her soul entrusted to any living creature.

Whilst I was treating with her in the

matter of my charge she would often make such digressions, either expressly to gain time and not to feel pressed by that I asked of her, or because it is her natural way. Then would she excuse herself, saying, "Master Ambassador, you will say of the tales that I am telling you that they are mere gullery. See what it is to have to do with old women such as I am." Then she returned to the subject of her talk to which I led her back, pressing her for an answer. She said to me, "I am between Scylla and Charibdis." She knows all the ancient histories, and one can say nothing to her on which she will not make some apt comment. She told me that it was reported that she had never read anything but the works of Calvin. She swore to me that she had never seen one, but that she had seen the ancient Fathers, and had taken great pleasure in them; all the more because later writers are full of disputes and strivings, and the others have only the good intent of rendering service and profit to God....

Having told her at some point that she was well advertised of everything that happened in the world, she replied that her hands were very long by nature...whereupon she drew off her glove and showed me her hand, which is very long and more than mine by more than three broad fingers. It was formerly very beautiful, but it is now very thin, although the skin is still most fair....It is a strange thing to see how lively she is in body and mind and nimble in everything she does. This day she was in very good humour and gay, and at my departure made me very good cheer, saluting all the gentlemen who were with me all together. She is a very great princess who knows everything....

The same day after dinner the Queen sent for me to go to her Council; and being in the Chamber of the Council a gentleman came to say that very soon the Queen would pass by with her ladies on her way to the dancing, and, that if I wished to see her pass, it was she who had sent him. I went there, and straightway she came out; and seeing me from afar she came towards me saying she had not thought to see me there, and that she was going to see the dancing, and demanded whether I did not wish to accompany her. I told her that I would do everything she commanded me, and bore her company. She herself sat in the gallery and made me sit by her.

She takes great pleasure in dancing and music. She told me that she entertained at least sixty musicians; in her youth she danced very well, and composed measures and music, and had played them herself and danced them. She takes such pleasure in it that when her Maids dance she follows the cadence with her head, hand and foot. She rebukes them if they do not dance to her liking, and without doubt she is a mistress of the art, having learnt in the Italian manner to dance high. She told me that they called her "the Florentine"....

10th January. This day the Queen sent her coaches according to her custom with a gentleman in ordinary called Sathus (?) and one of the four gentlemen servants....

I was conducted to her chamber, where I found her attired after her accustomed manner. She made me sit near her....

She spoke to me of the languages that she had learned, for she makes digressions very often, telling me that when she came to the Crown she knew six languages better than her own; and because I told her that it was great virtue in a princess, she said that it was no marvel to teach a woman to talk; it were far harder to teach her to hold her tongue.

Paul Hentzner

TRAVELS IN ENGLAND

Paul Hentzner (died 1623) was a native of Brandenburg who became a distinguished jurist and counselor to the Duke of Münsterburg. At the time of his travels in 1598 throughout Germany, Italy, France, and England, he was a tutor and companion to a young Silesian nobleman. His picture of Queen Elizabeth and the ritual of her court, which form a small part of the narrative of his travels, has become one of the standard sources of her reign. Originally written in Latin, Hentzner's impressions of England were translated at the request of Horace Walpole and printed for the Society of Antiquaries in 1797.

WE ARRIVED next at the royal palace of Greenwich, reported to have been originally built by Humphrey Duke of Gloucester, and to have received very magnificent additions from Henry VII. It was here Elizabeth, the present Queen, was born, and here she generally resides; particularly in summer, for the delightfulness of its situation. We were admitted...into the Presence-Chamber, hung with rich tapestry, and the floor after the English fashion, strewed with hay [rushes], through which the Queen commonly passes in her way to chapel: at the door stood a gentleman dressed in velvet, with a gold chain, whose office was to introduce to the Queen any person of distinction, that came to wait on her. It was Sunday, when there is usually the greatest attendance of nobility. In the same hall were the Archbishop of Canterbury, the Bishop of London, a great number of councillors of state, officers of the crown, and gentlemen, who waited the Queen's coming out; which she did from her own apartment, when it was time to go to prayers, attended in the following manner:

First went gentlemen, barons, earls, knights of the garter, all richly dressed and bareheaded; next came the chancellor, bearing the seals in a red-silk purse, between two—one of which carried the royal scepter, the other the sword of state, in a red scabbard studded with golden fleurs–de–lis, the point upwards—next came the Queen, in the sixty-fifth year of her age, as we were told, very majestic—her face oblong, fair, but wrinkled: her eyes small, yet black and pleasant; her nose a little hooked; her lips narrow; and her teeth black (a defect the English seem subject to, from their too great use of sugar); she had in her ears two pearls, with very rich drops; she wore false hair, and that red; upon her head she had a small crown; her bosom was uncovered, as all the English ladies have it, till they marry; and she had on a necklace of exceedingly fine jewels; her hands were small, her fingers long; and her stature neither tall nor low; her air was stately; her manner of speaking mild and obliging. That day she was dressed in white silk, bordered with pearls of the size of beans, and over it a

From *Paul Hentzner's Travels in England during the Reign of Queen Elizabeth*, trans. Horace, late Earl of Oxford (London, 1797), pp. 33-37.

mantle of black silk, shot with silver threads; her train was very long, the end of it borne by a marchioness; instead of a chain, she had an oblong collar of gold and jewels. As she went along in all this state and magnificence, she spoke very graciously, first to one, then to another, whether foreign ministers, or those who attended for different reasons, in English, French and Italian; for besides being well skilled in Greek, Latin, and the languages I have mentioned, she is mistress of Spanish, Scotch and Dutch. Whoever speaks to her, it is kneeling; now and then she raises some with her hand. While we were there, W. Slawata, a Bohemian baron, had letters to present to her; and she, after pulling off her glove, gave him her right hand to kiss, sparkling with rings and jewels, a mark of particular favor. Wherever she turned her face, as she was going along, everybody fell down on their knees. The ladies of the court followed next to her, very handsome and well shaped, and for the most part dressed in white; she was guarded on each side by the gentlemen pensioners, fifty in number, with gilt battleaxes. In the antichapel next to the hall where we were, petitions were presented to her, and she received them most graciously, which occasioned the acclamation of "Long live Queen Elizabeth!" She answered it with, "I thank you, my good people." In the chapel was excellent music; as soon as it and the service were over, which scarce exceeded half an hour, the Queen returned in the same state and order, and prepared to go to dinner. But while she was still at prayers, we saw her table set out with the following solemnity.

A gentleman entered the room bearing a rod, and along with him another who had a tablecloth, which, after they had both kneeled three times with the utmost veneration, he spread upon the table, and after kneeling again, they both retired. Then came two others, one with the rod again, the other with a saltcellar, a plate and bread; when they had kneeled, as the others had done, and placed what was brought upon the table, they too retired with the same ceremonies performed by the first. At last came an unmarried lady (we were told she was a countess) and along with her a married one, bearing a tasting knife; the former was dressed in white silk, who, when she had prostrated herself three times in the most graceful manner, approached the table, and rubbed the plates with bread and salt, with as much awe as if the Queen had been present. When they had waited there a little while, the yeomen of the guards entered, bareheaded, clothed in scarlet, with a golden rose upon their backs, bringing in at each turn a course of twenty-four dishes, served in plate, most of it gilt; these dishes were received by a gentleman in the same order they were brought, and placed upon the table, while the lady-taster gave to each of the guards a mouthful to eat of the particular dish he had brought for fear of any poison. During the time that this guard, which consists of the tallest and stoutest men that can be found in all England, being carefully selected for this service, were bringing dinner, twelve trumpets and two kettledrums made the hall ring for half an hour together. At the end of all this ceremony a number of unmarried ladies appeared, who, with particular solemnity, lifted the meat off the table and conveyed it into the Queen's inner and more private chamber, where, after she had chosen for herself, the rest goes to the ladies of the court.

The Queen dines and sups alone with very few attendants; and it is very seldom that anybody, foreigner or native, is admitted at that time, and then only at the intercession of somebody in power.

John Clapham

REIGN OF QUEEN ELIZABETH

John Clapham (1566–sometime after 1613) is a shadowy figure who was a member of Lord Burghley's household and later maintained himself as one of the six clerks of the Court of Chancery. Clapham, however, obviously did not regard himself as a civil servant but as a writer of "historical and poetical fantasies," the most enduring of which was his *Certain Observations Concerning the Life and Reign of Queen Elizabeth,* which was written within weeks of Gloriana's death but, oddly enough, was not published until 1952. Possibly Clapham had learned the dangers of inopportune publishing from the fate of John Hayward, who had spent over a year in prison for writing in 1599 about Henry IV's overthrow of Richard II. Certainly Clapham was aware that a historian's profession in the sixteenth century could be risky. In the preface to his *Historie of Great Britannie* (1606) he noted that "to set down truly the occurrences of the present or late times is found by experience to be a labor without thanks and now and then not without danger." Whatever else can be said about Clapham's portrait of the Queen, the strength of Elizabeth's personality was still strong in his memory, as it was for all his generation—a fact that must have been difficult for James I.

TO FLATTER princes, while they be alive, is a matter ordinary, as also it is to reprove them being dead. But for mine own part, although myself, among many others, have tasted the fruits of her peaceable government, under which I was born and have spent the rest of my life hitherto, yet will I not spare to write plainly and truly, according to my knowledge, of things past and yet fresh in remembrance, as a man void of fear, partiality, and all private respects....

I will address myself to my former purpose and proceed with the particular description of the Queen's disposition and natural gifts of mind and body, wherein she either matched or excelled all the princes of her time; as being of a great spirit, yet tempered with moderation; in adversity never diverted; in prosperity not altogether serene; affable to her subjects, but always with due regard of the greatness of her estate, by reason whereof she was both loved and feared. In her latter time, when she showed herself in public, she was always magnificent in apparel, supposing haply thereby that the eyes of her people, being dazzled with the glittering aspect of those accidental ornaments would not so easily discern the marks of age and decay of natural beauty. And she came abroad the more seldom, to make her presence the more

From John Clapham, *Elizabeth of England: Certain Observations Concerning the Life and Reign of Queen Elizabeth,* ed. E.P. Read and C. Read (Philadelphia: University of Pennsylvania Press, 1951), pp. 67, 85-90. Reprinted by permission of the publisher.

grateful and applauded by the multitude, to whom things rarely seen are in manner as new.

She suffered not at any time any suitor to depart discontented from her; yet he held himself satisfied with her manner of speech, which gave hope of success in a second attempt. And it was noted in her that she seldom or never denied any suit that was moved unto her, how unfit so ever to be granted, but the suitor received the answer of denial by some other; a thankless office and commonly performed by persons of greatest place, who ofttimes bear the blame of many things wherein themselves are not guilty, while no imputation must be laid upon the prince, and the vulgar sort for the most part discerning no more than what is personally apparent to their outward senses.

In granting offices, she used many delays, but after long suit she gave them voluntarily. The one perhaps she did for that she loved to be sued unto and to be gratified with rewards, and the other that she might not seem to yield by importunity and so lose the thanks that a good turn freely bestowed deserveth. She was accounted in her latter time to be very near and oversparing of expense; and yet, if the rewards which she sometimes gave of mere motion and grace had been bestowed of merit with due respect, they had doubtless purchased her the name of a very liberal prince. Howbeit (as unwilling, even in times of necessity, to overburden her subjects who had granted her many subsidies and lent her great sums of money), she was contented to sell some of her own lands and jewels to support the charge of the Irish war. Certain it is that some persons attending near about her would now and then abuse her favor and make sale of it, by taking bribes for such suits as she bestowed freely. Likewise purveyors and other officers of her household, under pretense of her service, would ofttimes for their own gain vex with many impositions the poorer sort of the inhabitants near the usual places of her residence. And although it be accounted as great a fault for a prince to be ill himself as to have ill officers about him, yet the consideration of her sex (she being a woman and wanting convenient means to understand the grievances of her poor but by report of others) may seem to carry some color of excuse. She was very rich in jewels, which had been given her by her subjects; for in times of progress there was no person that entertained her in his house but, besides his extraordinary charge in feasting her and her train, he bestowed a jewel upon her—a custom in former times begun by some of her special favorites that, having in good measure tasted of her bounty, did give her only of her own; though otherwise that kind of giving was not so pleasing to gentlemen of meaner quality.

During the long continuance of her government many secret treasons were practiced against her life, both by strangers and also by some of her own unnatural subjects; but God, that had ordained her to die as she lived, in peace, would not suffer them to prevail in their bad intentions. And Doctor Parry that had vowed to kill her, being alone with her in the garden at Richmond and then resolved to act that tragedy, was so daunted with the majesty of her presence, in which he then saw the image of her grandfather, King Henry VII, as himself confessed that his heart would not suffer his hand to execute that which he had resolved. And the selfsame day that the late Earl of Essex entered the city with divers noblemen and gentlemen of quality in a confused troop, when report was made unto her of the manner thereof, she being then at dinner seemed nothing moved therewith, but only said [that] He that had placed her on that seat would preserve her in it; and so she continued at her dinner, not showing any sign of fear or distraction of mind, nor omitting anything that day that she had been accustomed to do at other times: an argument of a religious resolution and great constancy in a woman and, as I think, but rarely to be found in men of more than ordinary spirits.

Touching those commendable qualities whereto, partly by nature and partly by education and industry, she had attained, there were few men that, when time and occasion served, could make better use or more show of them than herself. The Latin, Spanish, French, and Italian she could speak very elegantly, and she was able in all these languages to answer ambassadors on the sudden. Her manner of writing was somewhat obscure, and the style not vulgar, as being either learned by imitation of some author whom she delighted to read, or else affected for difference sake, that she might not write in such phrases as were commonly used. Of the Greek tongue also she was not altogether ignorant. She took pleasure in reading of the best and wisest histories, and some part of Tacitus' *Annals* she herself turned into English for her private exercise. She also translated Boethius, *De Consolatione Philosophiae,* and a treatise of Plutarch, *De Curiositate,* with diverse others. For her recreations, she used them moderately and wisely without touch to her reputation or offense to her people. She was in her diet very temperate, as eating but of few kinds of meat and those not compounded. The wine she drank was mingled with water, containing three parts more in quantity than the wine itself. Precise hours of refection she observed not, as never eating but when her appetite required it. In matters of recreation, as singing, dancing and playing upon instruments, she was not ignorant nor excellent: a measure which in things indifferent best beseemeth a prince.

She was of nature somewhat hasty but quickly appeased; ready there to show most kindness, where a little before she has been most sharp in reproving. Her greatest griefs of mind and body she either patiently endured or politely dissembled. I have heard it credibly reported that, not long before her death, she was divers times troubled with gout in her fingers whereof she would never complain, as seeming better pleased to be thought insensible of the pain than to acknowledge the disease. And she would often show herself abroad at public spectacles, even against her own liking, to no other end but that the people might the better perceive her ability of body and good disposition, where otherwise in respect of her years they might perhaps have doubted; so jealous was she to have her natural defects discovered for diminishing her reputation. As for flatterers, it is certain that she had many too near her, and was well contented to hear them. Howbeit, though it be a great fault in princes to endure such kind of persons about them, yet it is more tolerable in them to be flattered and praised sometimes for such virtues as they have not than to be hated and despised for known vices.

Sir Robert Naunton

FRAGMENTA REGALIA

Robert Naunton (1563-1635) was a highly successful, if minor, politician who succeeded in surviving every court upheaval of the late Elizabethan and early Stuart period. Originally a protégé of the Earl of Essex, he was groomed as a diplomat and was sent on mission to Denmark by James I. Naunton entered Parliament in 1606, was knighted in 1614, and became Master of Requests two years later. He was appointed Secretary of State in 1617-1618 and finally was made Master of the Court of Wards in 1623. He left an unpublished description of the principal statesmen and courtiers of Elizabeth's reign, and though it is obviously partial to the Earl of Essex, it is an astute commentary on court life under Elizabeth and on her management of those on whom she depended for government and security. Published first in 1641 under the title of *Fragmenta Regalia,* in subsequent editions its title was expanded.

THE PRINCIPAL note of her reign will be that she ruled much by faction and parties, which she herself both made, upheld and weakened, as her own great judgment advised; for I do dissent from the common and received opinion that my Lord of Leicester was absolute and alone in her grace. And, although I come somewhat short of the knowledge of these times, yet, that I may not err or shoot at random, I know it from assured intelligence that it was not so; for proof whereof, amongst many (that [I] could present) I will both relate a story, and therein a known truth, and it was thus.

Bowyer, the gentleman of the Black Rod, being charged by her express command to look precisely to all admissions in the Privy Chamber, one day stayed a very gay captain (and a follower of my Lord of Leicester) from entrance, for that he was neither well–known nor a sworn servant of the Queen. At which repulse, the gentleman (bearing high on my Lord's favor) told him, that he might, perchance, procure him a discharge. Leicester coming to the contestation said publicly, which was none of his wonted speeches, that he [Bowyer] was a knave and should not long continue in his office; and so turning about to go to the Queen, Bowyer, who was a bold gentleman and well-beloved, stepped before him and fell at her majesty's feet, relates the story and humbly craves her grace's pleasure, and in such a manner as if he had demanded whether my Lord of Leicester was king or her majesty queen. Whereunto she replied (with her wonted oath—"God's death"), "My Lord, I have wished you well, but my favor is not so locked up for you that others shall not

From Sir Robert Naunton, *Fragmenta Regalia, or Observations on Queen Elizabeth's Times and Favourites, with Portraits and Views* (London, 1797), pp. 82-84.

participate thereof; for I have many servants unto whom I have, and will, at my pleasure, bequeath my favor, and likewise resume the same; and if you think to rule here, I will take a course to see you forthcoming. I will have here but one mistress, and no master, and look that no ill happen to him, lest it be severely required at your hands." Which so quailed my Lord of Leicester that his fained humility was, long after, one of his best virtues.

II. ELIZABETH SPEAKS FOR HERSELF

THE QUEEN'S PUBLIC ADDRESSES

Elizabeth was a master of the spoken word, which she used liberally to obscure and defuse a political crisis, to cement her relations with her subjects and particularly with that difficult and often unruly body—the two houses of Parliament—and finally to reveal her mind about the nature of kingship and her royal authority. Throughout her reign she was at odds with Parliament over four interrelated issues: her failure to marry and beget an heir; her refusal to name a successor; her reluctance to permit the execution of her first-cousin-once-removed, Mary Queen of Scotland; and her distaste for changing the established religion of the land. The following extracts cover her entire reign; except for the last two examples they involve her running controversy with Parliament and her ability to say no in the face of overwhelming pressure.

To the House of Commons, 1559

(in answer to its request that she marry)

AND, DURING the continuance of this Parliament, the knights and burgesses of the lower house (doubtful whether of themselves or set unto it by some lofty spirit) made suit to the Queen that they might have access to her presence, to move a matter unto her which they esteemed of great importance for the general state of all the realm. This was granted, and a certain time of audience appointed; upon which day she came forth into the great gallery at Whitehall, richly furnished in attire, and honorably attended. And, when she was placed in her royal seat, the Commons of the Parliament were brought before her. Here the Speaker delivered a set oration....The sum and substance of that which he said contained a suit that she would be pleased to dispose herself to marriage, as well for her own comfort and contentment, as for the assurance to the realm by her royal issue; that, if succession to the Crown were by this means certainly known, not only those dangers should be prevented which, after her death, might fall upon the state, but those also which, in the meantime, did threaten herself; and that, thereby, as well the fears of her faithful subjects and friends, as the ambitious hopes of her enemies, should clean be cut off.

The Queen, after a sweet graced silence, with a princely countenance and voice, and with a gesture somewhat quick but not violent, returned answer,

From Sir John Hayward, *Annals*, pp. 30-33.

that she gave them great thanks (as she saw great cause) for the love and care which they did express as well towards her person as the whole state of the realm; "and first" (said she) "for the manner of your petition, I like it well, and take it in good part, because it is simple, without any limitation, either of person or place. If it had been otherwise; if you had taken upon you to confine, or rather to bind, my choice, to draw my love to your liking, to frame my affections according unto your fantasies, I must have disliked it very much; for as, generally, the will desireth not a larger liberty in my case then in this, so had it been a great presumption for you to direct, to limit, to command me herein, to whom you are bound in duty to obey.

"Concerning the substance of your suit, since my years of understanding, since I was first able to take consideration of myself, I have hitherto made choice of a single life, which hath best, I assure you, contented me, and, I trust, hath been most acceptable to God.... Nevertheless, if any of you suspect that, in case it shall please God hereafter to change my purpose, I will determine something to the prejudice of the realm, put the jealousy out of your heads, for I assure [you]...I will never conclude anything in that matter which shall be hurtful to the realm, for the preservation and prosperity whereof as a loving mother I will never spare to spend my life. And upon whomsoever my choice shall fall he shall be as careful for your preservation —I will not say as myself, for I cannot undertake for another as for myself—but my will and best endeavour shall not fail that he shall be as careful for you as myself. And, albeit it shall please God that I still persevere in a virgin's state, yet you must not fear but He will so work, both in my heart and in your wisdoms, that provision shall be made, in convenient time, whereby the realm shall not remain destitute of an heir who may be a fit governor, and peradventure, more beneficial than such offspring as I should bring forth, for, although I be careful of your well-doings, and ever purpose so to be, yet may my issue degenerate, and grow out of kind. The dangers which you fear are neither so certain, nor of such nature, but you may repose yourselves upon the providence of God, and the good provisions of the state. Wits curious in casting things to come are often hurtful, for that the affairs of this world are subject to so many accidents that seldom doth that happen which the wisdom of men doth seem to foresee. As for me, it shall be sufficient that a marble stone shall declare that a Queen, having lived and reigned so many years, died a virgin. And here I end, and take your coming in very good part, and again give hearty thanks to you all; yet more for your zeal and good meaning, than for the matter of your suit."

To the Scottish Ambassador, 1561

*(in answer to his suggestion that she name
Mary Queen of Scots the legal successor)*

THE QUEEN of Scots, in a short time after her arrival [in Scotland], an Ambassador into England to salute the Queen, to declare her good affection, and the desire that she had to preserve peace and friendship between them. He brought also letters from the nobility of Scotland containing a ...request that...she would declare, by act of Parliament, that, next to herself,

From Sir John Hayward, *Annuals*, pp. 78-85.

and such issue as she might bring forth, heir Queen was heir to the crown of England. The Ambassador enlarged by many arguments that this request was both reasonable in itself and exceedingly beneficial to both the realms; that it was expected that none should be more forward therein than the Queen herself, to testify thereby her love to their Queen, as being the nearest unto her in blood.

To this the Queen, with countenance full of comely majesty, made answer.... [There were many reasons, she said, why it would be dangerous for her to do as the ambassador requested.]...

"First, for that I am not ignorant how dangerous it is to blow these coals. I have had good reason methinks always to forbear to move disputation and doubts concerning this matter. The controversy of marriage, allowed or void, the question of issue, lawful or unlawful, hath been so often, and by so many wits, canvassed on both sides, whilst every man favoreth one party or another, that, for this cause, I have been hitherto the less forward to marriage. I was once married to this realm at my coronation, in token whereof I wear this ring; howsoever things stand, I will be Queen of England so long as I live; after my death let them succeed to whom in right it shall appertain. If that be your Queen (as I know not who should be before her), I will not be against it. I will be no impediment unto her. If there by any law against her title, I am ignorant thereof. But this I know, that in succession of kingdoms, the fundamental law of the crown of the realm, the immutable law of nature and of nations (which proceedeth by propinquity of blood) is more regarded than either secret implications or express cautions of positive laws.

"For that you assume, in the second place, that, upon this declaration, the friendship would be more firm between us, I fear you are deceived; I fear it would be rather an origin of hatred. It is natural, indeed, for parents to favor the succession of their children, to be careful for it, to provide for it, to assure it by all means unto them, because nature is of force to extinguish both the cause and the care of other respects. But, in more distant degrees it is almost peculiar to kings to be jealous of those who are in next expectation to succeed. Yea, Charles VII, King of France, how was he affected to Louis XI? Again, how was Louis affected toward Charles VIII? or how was Francis of late toward Henry II? Is it like, then, that I shall bear any better affection toward one that is no nearer in kindred to me than your Queen, when she shall be once declared mine heir? Is it like that I shall be well pleased in regard of her, with continual view of mine own hearse? Add hereto, that which I esteem of greatest moment, I am well acquainted with the nature of this people; I know how easily they dislike the present state of affairs; I know what nimble eyes they bear to the next succession; I know it to be natural that more (as the saying is) do adore the rising than the falling sun. To omit other examples, I have learned this by experience of mine own times. When my sister Mary was Queen, what prayers were made by many to see me placed in her seat; with what earnest desire were they carried for my advancement? I am not ignorant with what dangers men would have adventured the event of their counsels, if my will had been applicable to their desires. Now happily, the same men are not of the same mind. But as children, which, dreaming that apples are given them, whilst they sleep are exceedingly glad, but waking and finding themselves deceived of their hope they fall to crying, so some of them, who did highly favor me when I was called Elizabeth, who, if I did cast a kind countenance upon them, did forthwith conceive that, so soon as I should attain the crown, they should be rewarded rather according to their desires than their deserts, now, finding their lot not answerable to their hope (because no prince is able to fill the insatiable gulf of men's desires), they would happily be content with another change, upon possibility thereby to better their state. Now then, if the affections of our people grow faint, if their minds change upon bearing a moderate hand in distributions of rewards and gifts, or upon some other cause more light, what may we look for when evil-minded men shall have a foreign prince appointed the certain successor to the crown, to whom they may carry all their complaints? In how great danger shall I be (do you think) when a prince so powerful, so near unto me, shall be declared my successor? To whom so much strength as I shall add by confirming her succession, so much security shall I detract from myself. Neither can the danger be avoided by any assurances and bands of law, for that princes, in hope of a kingdom, will not easily contain themselves within the limits of any law. Assuredly, if my successor were known to the world, I would never esteem my state to be safe.''

To a delegation of the House of Commons, 1563
(in answer to a petition that she name a successor)

The problem for Elizabeth was that she had been desperately ill, which was regarded by all as a "dreadful warning." Furthermore, Mary of Scotland was not only her blood heir and a tool in the hands of France and Spain, but—even worse—was a Catholic.

THE WEIGHT and greatness of this matter might cause in me, being a woman wanting both wit and memory, some fear to speak and bashfulness besides, a thing appropriate to my sex. But yet, the princely seat and kingly throne wherein God (though unworthy) hath constituted me, maketh these two causes to seem little in mine eyes, though grievous perhaps to your ears, and boldeneth me to say somewhat in this matter, which I mean only to touch but not presently to answer. For this so great a demand needeth both great and grave advice. I read of a philosopher, whose deeds upon this occasion I remember better than his name, who always, when he was required to give answer in any hard question of school points, would rehearse over his alphabet before he would proceed to any further answer therein: not for that he could not presently have answered, but to have his wit the riper and better sharpened to answer the matter withal. If he, a common man, but in matters of school took such delay, the better to show his eloquent tale, great cause may justly move me in this so great a matter, touching the benefit of this realm and the safety of you all, to defer mine answer till some other time; wherein, I assure you, the consideration of my own safety (although I thank you for the great care that you seem to have thereof) shall be little in comparison of that great regard that I mean to have of the safety and surety of you all.

And though God of late seemed to touch me, rather like one that He chastised than one that He punished, and

From John E. Neale, *Elizabeth and Her Parliaments* (London: Jonathan Cape, Ltd., 1953), Vol. I, pp. 107-109. Reprinted by permission of the publisher.

though death possessed almost every joint of me, so as I wished then that the feeble thread of life, which lasted (methought) all too long, might by Cloe's hand have quietly been cut off; yet desired I not then life (as I have some witnesses here) so much for mine own safety as for yours. For I knew that in exchanging of this reign I should have enjoyed a better reign, where residence is perpetual. There needs no boding of my bane [i.e., to speak of my death] I know now as well as I did before that I am mortal. I know also that I must seek to discharge myself of that great burden that God hath laid upon me. For of them to whom much is committed much is required. Think not that I, that in other matters have had convenient care of you all, will in this matter, touching the safety of myself and you all, be careless. For I know that this matter toucheth me much nearer than it doth you all, who, if the worst happen, can lose but your bodies; but if I take not that convenient care that it behoveth me to have therein, I hazard to lose both body and soul.

And though I am determined in this so great and weighty a matter to defermine answer till some other time because I will not in so deep a matter wade with so shallow a wit; yet have I thought good to use these few words, as well to show you that I am neither careless nor unmindful of your safety in this case—as I trust you likewise do not forget that by me you were delivered whilst you were hanging on the bough ready to fall into the mud, yea to be drowned in the dung, neither yet [do you forget] the promise which you have here made concerning your duties and due obedience, wherewith, I assure you, I mean to charge you—as further to let you understand that I neither mislike any of your requests herein, nor the great care that you seem to have of the surety and safety of yourselves in this matter. Lastly—because I will discharge some restless heads, in whose brains the needless hammers beat with vain judgment, that I should mislike this their petition—I say that of the matter and sum thereof I like and allow very well. As to the circumstances, if any be, I mean upon further advice further to answer. And so I assure you all that, though after my death you may have many stepdames, yet shall you never have a more natural mother than I mean to be unto you all.

To a delegation of both houses, Nov. 1566

*(in answer to another demand that she name
a successor and select a mate)*

Elizabeth was particularly angered by Parliament's suggestion that her refusal stemmed from selfishness on her part, and she commenced her speech with a fiery introduction.

WAS I not born in the realm? Were my parents born in any foreign country? Is there any cause I should alienate myself from being careful over this country? Is not my kingdom here? Whom have I oppressed? Whom have I enriched to other's harm? What turmoil have I made in this Commonwealth that I should be suspected to have no regard to the same? How have I gov-

From John E. Neale, *Elizabeth and Her Parliaments,* Vol. I, pp. 147-150. Reprinted by permission of the publisher.

erned since my reign? I will be tried by envy itself. I need not to use many words, for my deeds do try me....

Well, the matter whereof they would have made their petition (as I am informed) consisteth in two points — in my marriage and in the limitation of the succession of the Crown, wherein my marriage was first placed, as for manner's sake. I did send them answer by my Council I would marry (although of mine own disposition I was not inclined thereunto). But that was not accepted or credited, although spoken by their Prince. And yet I used so many words that I could say no more: and were it not now I had spoken those words, I would never speak them again. I will never break the word of a prince, spoken in a public place, for my honour's sake. And therefore I say again, I will marry as soon as I can conveniently, if God take not him away with whom I mind to marry, or myself, or else some other great let happen. I can say no more, except the party were present. And I hope to have children, otherwise I would never marry.

A strange order of petitioners, that will make a request and cannot be otherwise ascertained but by their Prince's word, and yet will not believe it when it is spoken! But they (I think) that moveth the same will be as ready to mislike him with whom I shall marry, as they are now to move it. And then it will appear they nothing meant it. I thought they would have been rather ready to have given me thanks than to have made any new request for the same. There hath been some that have ere this said unto me they never required more than that they might once hear me say I would marry. Well, there was never so great a treason but might be covered under as fair a pretense....

The second point was the limitation of the succession of the crown: wherein was nothing said for my safety but only for themselves. A strange thing that the foot should direct the head in so weighty a cause; which cause hath been so dili-

gently weighed by us, for that it toucheth us more than them. I am sure there was not one of them that ever was a second person, as I have been, and have tasted of the practices against my sister....

I have conferred before this time with those that are well learned, and have asked their opinions touching the limitation of succession....

It is said, I am no divine. Indeed, I studied nothing else but divinity till I came to the crown; and then I gave myself to the study of that which was meet for government, and am not ignorant of stories wherein appeareth what hath fallen out for ambition of kingdoms — as in Spain, Naples, Portugal, and at home; and what cocking hath been between the father and the son for the same. You would have a limitation of succession. Truly, if reason did not subdue will in me, I would cause you to deal in it, so pleasant a thing it should be unto me. But I stay it for your benefit. For if you should have liberty to treat of it, there be so many competitors — some kinfolks, some servants, and some tenants; some would speak for their master, and some for their mistress, and every man for his friend — that it would be an occasion of a greater charge than a subsidy. And if my will did not yield to reason, it should be that thing I would gladliest desire to see you deal in....

And though I be a woman, yet I have as good a courage, answerable to my place, as ever my father had. I am your anointed Queen. I will never be by violence constrained to do anything. I thank God I am endued with such qualities that if I were turned out of the realm in my petticoat, I were able to live in any place in Christendom. Your petition is to deal in the limitation of the succession. At this present it is not convenient; nor never shall be without some peril unto you and certain danger unto me. But were it not for your peril, at this time I would give place, notwithstanding my danger.... But as soon as there may be a convenient time, and that it may be done with least peril unto you — although never without great danger unto me — I will deal therein for your safety, and offer it unto you as your Prince and head, without request; for it is monstrous that the feet should direct the head.

To Parliament, March 29, 1585

(in answer to a Puritan effort to persuade her to "reform" the Church of England)

MY LORDS and ye of the lower house, my silence must not injure the owner so much as to suppose a substitute sufficient to render you the thanks that my heart yieldeth you—not so much for the safekeeping of my life (for which your care appeareth so manifest) as for the neglecting your private future peril, not regarding other way than my present state. No prince herein, I confess, can be surer tied or faster bound than I am, with the link of your good will; and can for that but yield a heart and head to seek forever all your best. Yet one matter toucheth me so near as I may not overskip: religion, the ground on which all other matters ought to take root, and being corrupted may mar all the tree. And that there be some faultfinders with the order of the clergy, which so may make a slander to myself and the church, whose overruler God hath made me, whose negligence cannot be excused, if any schisms or errors heretical were suffered.

Thus much I must say, that some faults and negligences may grow and be (as in all other great charges it happeneth) and what vocation without? All which if you my lords of the clergy do not amend, I mean to depose you. Look you therefore well to your charges; this may be amended without heedless or open exclamation. I am supposed to have many studies, but most philosophical I must yield this to be true, that I suppose few that be no professors have read more. And I need not tell you that I am so simple that I understand not, nor so forgetful that I remember not: and yet amongst my many volumes, I hope God's book hath not been my seldomest lectures, in which we find that, which by reason (for my part) we ought to believe....

And so you see that you wrong me too much, if any such there be as doubt my coldness in that behalf. For if I were not persuaded that mine were the true way of God's will, God forbid I should live to prescribe it to you....I see many overbold with God Almighty, making too many subtle scannings of His blessed will, as lawyers do with human testaments. The presumption is so great as I may not suffer it. Yet mind I not hereby to animate Romanists—which what adversaries they be to mine estate is sufficiently known—nor tolerate newfangledness. I mean to guide them both by God's true rule. In both parts by perils, and of the latter I must pronounce them dangerous to kingly rule, to have every man according to his own censure to make a doom of the validity and privity of his

From Ralph Holinshed, *Chronicles of England, Scotland, and Ireland* (London, 1807-1808), Vol. IV, pp. 588-589.

prince's government, and with a common veil and cover of God's word, whose followers must not be judged but by private men's exposition. God defend you from such a ruler that so evil will guide you. Now I conclude that your love and care neither is nor shall be bestowed upon a careless prince, but such as for your good will passeth as little for this world as who careth least. With thanks for your free subsidy, a manifest show of the abundance of your good wills, the which I assure you, but to be employed to your weal, I could be better pleased to return than receive.

To a delegation of both houses, November 12, 1586

(in answer to a petition begging her to permit the execution of Mary Queen of Scots)

Mary had been in custody since 1568 and was regarded by Parliament as a constant threat to the Queen's life, to the Protestant faith, and to the internal peace of the kingdom.

THE BOTTOMLESS graces and immeasurable benefits bestowed upon me by the Almighty are, and have been, such as I must not only acknowledge them but admire them, accounting them as well miracles as benefits; not so much in respect of His divine majesty, with whom nothing is more common than to do things rare and singular, as in regard of our weakness, who cannot sufficiently set forth His wonderful works and graces, which to me have been so many, so diversely folded and embroidered one upon another, as in no sort I am able to express them. And although there liveth not any that may more justly acknowledge themselves infinitely bound unto God than I, whose life He hath miraculously preserved at sundry times (beyond my merit) from a multitude of perils and dangers, yet is not that the cause for which I count myself the deepliest bound to give Him my humblest thanks, or to yield Him great recognition; but this which I shall tell you hereafter, which will deserve the name of wonder, if rare things and seldom seen be worthy of account. Even this it is that as I came to the crown with the willing hearts of my subjects, so do I now after eight and twenty years' reign, perceive in you no diminution of good wills, which if happily I should want, well might I breathe but never think I lived.

And now, albeit I find my life hath been full dangerously sought, and death contrived by such as no desert procured, yet am I therein so clear from malice (which hath the property to make men glad at the fails and faults of their foes, and make them seem to do for other causes when rancor is the ground) as I

From Ralph Holinshed, *Chronicles,* Vol. IV, pp. 933-935.

protest it is and hath been my grievous thought that one, not different in sex, of like estate, and my near kin, should fall into so great a crime. Yea, I had so little purpose to pursue her with any color of malice that, as it is now unknown to some of my lords here (for now I will play the blab), I secretly wrote her a letter upon the discovery of sundry treasons, that if she would confess them, and privately acknowledge them by her letters to myself, she never should need be called for them into so public question. Neither did I [have] it of mind to circumvent her, for then I knew as much as she could confess, and so did I write. And if even yet—now that the matter is made but too apparent—I thought she truly would repent (as perhaps she would easily appear in outward show to do) and that for her, none other would take the matter upon them; or that we were but as two milkmaids with pails upon our arms, or that there were no more dependency upon us but mine own life were only in danger, and not the whole estate of your religion and well doings, I protest (wherein you may believe me, for though I may have many vices, I hope I have not accustomed my tongue to be an instrument of untruth) I would most willingly pardon and remit this offense.

Or if by my death other nations and kingdoms might truly say that this realm had attained an ever prosperous and flourishing estate, I would (I assure you) not desire to live, but gladly give my life to the end my death might procure you a better prince. And for your sakes it is that I desire to live, to keep you from a worse. For as for me, I assure you, I find no great cause I should be fond to live; I take no such pleasure in it that I should much wish it: nor conceive such terror in death that I should greatly fear it....I have had good experience and trial of this world. I know what it is to be a subject, what to be a sovereign, what to have good neighbors, and sometime meet evil willers. I have found treason in trust, seen great benefits little regarded, and instead of gratefulness, courses of purpose to cross.

These former remembrances, present feeling and future expectation of evils, I say have made me think. An evil is much the better, the less while it endureth: and so them happiest that are soonest hence: and taught me to bear with a better mind these treasons than is common to my sex —yea, with a better heart perhaps than is in some men....And now, as touching their treasons and conspiracies, together with the contriver of them, I will not so prejudice myself and this my realm as to say or think that I might not, without the last statute [of 1584-85], by the ancient laws of this land have proceeded against her....But since it is made and in the force of a law, I thought good, in that which might concern her, to proceed according thereunto, rather than by course of common law; wherein, if you the judges have not deceived me or that the books you brought me were not false (which God forbid), I might as justly have tried her by the ancient laws of the land.

But you lawyers are so nice in sifting and scanning every word and letter, that many times you stand more upon form than matter, upon syllables than sense of the law. For in the strictness and exact following of common form, she must have been indicted in Staffordshire, have holden up her hand at the bar, and been tried by a jury: a proper course forsooth, to deal in that manner with one of her estate! I thought it better therefore, for avoiding of these and more absurdities, to commit the cause to the inquisition of a good number of the greatest and most noble personages of this realm, of the judges and others of good account whose sentence I must approve. And all little enough. For we princes, I tell you, are set on stages, in the sight and view of all the world duly observed: the eyes of many behold our actions; a spot is soon spied in our garments; a blemish quickly noted in our doings. It behoveth us therefore to be careful that our proceedings be just and honorable.

But I must tell you one thing more, that in this last act of Parliament you have brought me unto a narrow straight, that I must give direction for her death, which cannot be to me but a most grievous and irksome burden. And lest you might mistake mine absence from this Parliament...for that amongst many some may be evil, yet hath it not been the doubt of any such danger or occasion that kept me from thence; but only the great grief to hear this cause spoken of, especially that such a one of state and kin should need so open a declaration, and that this nation should be so spotted with blots of disloyalty....And even now could I tell you that which would make you sorry. It is a secret, and yet I will tell it you; although it is known I have the property to keep counsel but too well oftentimes to mine own peril. It is not long since my eyes did see it written that an oath was taken within few days either to kill me or to be hanged themselves; and that to be performed ere one month were ended. Hereby I see your danger in me, and neither can nor will be so unthankful or careless of your consciences as not provide for your safety.

I am not unmindful of your oath,... manifesting your great good wills and affections, taken and entered into upon good conscience and true knowledge of the guilt [of Mary Stuart], for the safety of my person, and conservation of my life....Which as I do acknowledge as a perfect argument of your true hearts and great zeal to my safety, so shall my bond be stronger tied to greater care for all your good. But for as much as this matter is rare, weighty and of great consequence, I think you do not look for any present resolution. The rather, for that as it is not my manner in matters of far less moment to give speedy answer without due consideration, so in this of such importance, I think it very requisite with earnest prayer to beseech His divine majesty, so to illuminate my understanding and inspire me with His grace, as I may do and determine that which shall serve to the establishment of His church, preservation of your estates and prosperity of this commonwealth under my charge. Wherein—for that I know delay is dangerous—you shall have with all convenience our resolution delivered by our message. And whatever any prince may merit of their subjects, for their approved testimony of their unfained sincerity, either by governing justly, void of all partiality, or sufferance of any injuries done—even to the poorest—that do I assuredly promise inviolably to perform, for requital of your so many deserts.

To a delegation of both houses, Nov. 24, 1586

(begging a clear answer to the preceding petition)

In the previous address Elizabeth had asked for time to think before answering Parliament's request to have Mary executed. Twelve days later a delegation of Lords and Commons was back with a second petition, asking for a clear answer from the Queen. What they got is recorded here.

From Ralph Holinshed, *Chronicles,* Vol. IV, pp. 938–940.

IHAVE STRIVED more this day than ever in my life whether I should speak or use silence. If I speak and not complain, I shall dissemble: if I hold my peace, your labor taken were full vain. For me to make my moan were strange and rare, for I suppose you shall find few that for their own particular will cumber you with such a care. Yet such I protest hath been my greedy desire and hungry will that of your consultation might have fallen out some other means to work my safety joined with your assurance (than that for which you are become such earnest suitors) as I protest, I must needs use complaint—though not of you, but unto you, and of the cause. For that I do perceive by your advices, prayers and desires, there falleth out this accident, that only my injurer's bane [death] must be my life's surety....

And since now it is resolved, that my surety cannot be established without a princess' end, I have just cause to complain that I, who have in my time pardoned so many rebels, winked at so many treasons, and either not produced them or altogether slipped them over with silence, should now be forced to this proceeding against such a person. I have besides, during my reign, seen and heard many opprobrious books and pamphlets against me, my realm and state, accusing me to be a tyrant....What will they not now say, when it shall be spread that for the safety of her life, a maiden Queen could be content to spill the blood even of her own kinswoman? I may therefore full well complain that any man should think me given to cruelty—whereof I am so guiltless and innocent as I should slander God if I should say He gave me so vile a mind. Yea, I protest; I am so far from it that for mine own life I would not touch her. Neither hath my care been so much bent how to prolong mine as how to preserve both—which I am right sorry is made so hard, yea so impossible.

I am not so void of judgment as not to see mine own peril; nor yet so ignorant as not to know it were in nature a foolish course to cherish a sword to cut mine own throat; nor so careless as not to weigh that my life daily is in hazard: but this I do consider, that many a man would put his life in danger for the safeguard of a king. I do not say that so will I, but I pray you think that I have thought upon it. But since so many have both written and spoken against me, I pray you give me leave to say somewhat for myself, and before you return to your countries [shires], let you know for what a one you have passed so careful thoughts. Wherein, as I think myself infinitely beholding unto you all that seek to preserve my life by all the means you may, so I protest unto you that there liveth no prince that ever shall be more mindful to requite so good deserts. And as I perceive you have kept your old wonts, in a general seeking of the lengthening of my days, so am I sure that I shall never requite it, unless I had as many lives as you all. But forever I will acknowledge it, while there is any breath left me. Although I may not justify, but may justly condemn my sundry faults and sins to God, yet for my care in this government, let me acquaint you with my intents.

When first I took the scepter, my title made me not forget the giver, and therefore [I] began as it became me, with such religion as both I was born in, bred in, and I trust shall die in. Although I was not simple as not to know what danger and peril so great an alteration might procure me, how many great princes of the contrary opinion would attempt all they might against me, and generally what enmity I should breed unto myself, which all I regarded not, knowing that He, for whose sake I did it, might and would defend me. For which it is that ever since I have been so dangerously prosecuted, as I rather marvel that I am, than muse that I should not be if it were not God's holy hand that continueth me beyond all other expectation. Then entered I further into the school of experience, bethinking what it fitted a king to do, and there I saw he scant was well furnished if either he lacked justice, temperance, magnanimity or judgment. As for the two latter, I will not boast (my sex doth not permit it), but for the two first, this dare I say: amongst my subjects I never knew a difference of person where right was one; nor never to my knowledge preferred for favor whom I thought not fit for worth; nor bent my ears to credit a tale that first was told me: nor was so rash to corrupt my judgment with my censure before I heard the cause. I will not say but many reports might fortune be brought me by such as might hear the case, whose partiality might mar sometime the matter: for we princes may not hear all ourselves. But this dare I boldly affirm: my verdict went ever with the truth of my knowledge. As full well wished Alcibiades his friend, that he should not give any answer till he had recited the letters of the alphabet, so have I not used over-sudden resolutions in matters that have touched me full near; you will say that with me, I think.

And therefore, as touching your counsels and consultations, I conceive them to be wise, honest and conscionable; so provident and careful for the safety of my life (which I wish no longer than may be for your good) that though I never can yield you of recompense your due, yet shall I endeavor myself to give you cause to think your goodwill not ill–bestowed, and strive to make myself worthy for such subjects. And now for your petition, I shall pray you for this present to content yourselves with an answer without answer. Your judgment I condemn not, neither do I mistake your reasons, but pray you to accept my thankfulness, excuse my doubtfulness, and take in good part my answer answerless. Where–in I attribute not so much to mine own judgment but that I think many particular persons may go before me, though by my degree I go before them. Therefore, if I should say I would not do what you request, it might peradventure be more than I thought; and to say I would do it might perhaps breed peril of that you labor to preserve, being more than in your own wisdoms and discretions would seem convenient, circumstances of place and time being duly considered.

To the soldiers at Tilbury, August 18, 1588

(during the crisis of the Armada)

MY LOVING People, we have been persuaded by some that are careful of our safety, to take heed how we commit ourself to armed multitudes, for fear of treachery; but I assure you, I do not desire to live to distrust my faithful and loving people. Let tyrants fear. I have always so behaved myself, that under God, I have placed my chiefest strength and safeguard in the loyal hearts and goodwill of my subjects, and therefore I am come amongst you, as you see, at this time, not for my recreation and disport, but being resolved, in the midst and heat of the battle, to live or die amongst you all, to lay down for my God,

From a letter of Dr. Leonel Sharp to the Duke of Buckingham in *Cabala, sive Serinia Sacra, Mysteries of State and Government: in Letters of Illustrious Persons*...(London, 1663), p. 373.

and for my Kingdom, and for my People, my honor and my blood, even in the dust. I know I have the body but of a weak and feeble woman, but I have the heart and stomach of a King, and of a King of England too, and think foul scorn that Parma or Spain, or any Prince of Europe should dare to invade the borders of my Realm; to which, rather than any dishonor shall grow by me, I myself will take up arms. I myself will be your general, judge, and rewarder of every one of your virtues in the field. I know, already for your forwardness, you have deserved rewards and crowns; and we do assure you, in the word of a Prince, they shall be duly paid you.

To Parliament, Nov. 30, 1601

The Queen's "Golden Speech"

The Queen spoke in answer to mounting criticism of her government's economic policies and the accusation that her administration was corrupt. Her address is far more than a promise to reform; it was Elizabeth's swan song to almost forty years of ruling.

MR. SPEAKER, We have heard your declaration and perceive your care of our state, by falling into the consideration of a grateful acknowledgment of such benefits as you have received; and that your coming is to present thanks unto us, which I accept with no less joy than your loves can have desire to offer such a present.

I do assure you, there is no prince that loveth his subjects better, or whose love can countervail our love. There is no jewel, be it of never so rich a price, which I set before this jewel; I mean your love. For I do more esteem it than any treasure or riches, for that we know how to prize, but love and thanks I count invaluable.

And, though God hath raised me high, yet this I count the glory of my crown, that I have reigned with your loves. This makes me that I do not so much rejoice, that God hath made me to be a queen, as to be a queen over so thankful a people.

Therefore, I have cause to wish nothing more than to content the subjects, and that is a duty which I owe. Neither do I desire to live longer days than I may see your prosperity; and that's my only desire.

And as I am that person that still (yet under God) hath delivered you, so I trust (by the Almighty Power of God) that I still shall be His instrument to preserve you from envy, peril, dishonor, shame, tyranny and oppression; partly by means of your intended helps, which we take very acceptably, because it manifests the largeness of your loves and loyalty to your sovereign.

Of myself I must say this: I was never any greedy scraping grasper, nor a straight, fast-holding prince, nor yet a

From Hayward Townshend, *Historical Collections...* (London, 1680), pp. 263-266.

waster. My heart was never set on worldly goods, but only for my subjects' good. What you do bestow on me, I will not hoard it up, but receive it to bestow on you again. Yea, my own properties I count yours, and to be expended for your good; and your eyes shall see the bestowing of all for your good. Therefore, render unto them from me, I beseech you, Mr. Speaker, such thanks as you imagine my heart yieldeth but my tongue cannot express.

[Note, all this while we kneeled. Where-upon her majesty said: "Mr. Speaker, I would wish you and the rest to stand up, for I shall yet trouble you with longer speech." So we all stood up, and she went on with her speech, saying:]

Mr. Speaker,

You give me thanks, but I doubt me that I have more cause to thank you all than you me. And I charge you go thank them of the Lower House from me. For had I not received a knowledge from you, I might have fallen into the lapse of an error, only for lack of true information.

Since I was Queen, yet did I never put my pen unto any grant but that, upon pretext and semblance made unto me, it was both good and beneficial to the subject in general, though a private profit to some of my ancient servants who had deserved well at my hands. But the contrary being found by experience, I am exceedingly beholding to such subjects as would move the same at the first. And I am not so simple to suppose but that there are some of the Lower House whom these grievances never touched. And for them, I think they spake out of zeal for their countries, and not out of spleen or malevolent affection as being parties grieved. And I take it exceeding gratefully from them, because it gives us to know that no respects or interests had moved them other than the minds they bear to suffer no diminution of our honour and our subjects' loves unto us. The zeal of which affection, tending to ease

my people and knit their hearts unto me, I embrace with a princely care, for (above all earthly treasure) I esteem my people's love more than which I desire not to merit.

That my grants should be grievous to my people and oppressions privileged under color of our patents, our kingly dignity shall not suffer it. Yea, when I heard it I could give no rest unto my thoughts until I had reformed it.

Shall they think to escape unpunished, that have thus oppressed you and have been respectless of their duty and regardless of our honor? No, Mr. Speaker, I assure you, were it not more for conscience' sake than for any glory or increase of love that I desire these errors, troubles, vexations and oppressions done by these varlets and lewd persons, not worthy the name of subjects, should not escape without condign punishment. But I perceive they deal with me like physicians who, administering a drug, make it more acceptable by giving it a good aromatical savor, or when they give pills do gild them all over.

I have ever used to set the last Judgment Day before my eyes, as so to rule as I shall be judged to answer before a higher Judge, to whose judgment seat I do appeal: that never thought was cherished in my heart that tended not to my people's good. And now, if my kingly bounty have been abused, and my grants turned to the hurt of my people, contrary to my will and meaning, or if any in authority under me have neglected or perverted what I have committed to them, I hope God will not lay their culps and offenses to my charge; who though there were danger in repealing our grants, yet what danger would I not rather incur for your good than I would suffer them still to continue?

I know the title of a king is a glorious title. But assure yourself that the shining glory of princely authority hath not so dazzled the eyes of our understanding but that we well know and remember that we also are to yield an account of our actions before the great Judge.

To be a king and wear a crown is a thing more glorious to them that see it than it is pleasing to them that bear it. For myself, I was never so much enticed with the glorious name of a king, or royal authority of a queen, as delighted that God had made me His instrument to maintain His truth and glory, and to defend this kingdom (as I said) from peril, dishonor, tyranny and oppression.

There will never queen sit in my seat with more zeal to my country, care for my subjects, and that sooner with willingness will venture her life for your good and safety, than myself. For it is not my desire to live nor reign longer than my life and reign shall be for your good. And though you have had, and may have, many princes more mighty and wise sitting in this state, yet you never had, or shall have, any that will be more careful and loving.

Shall I ascribe anything to myself and my sexly weakness? I were not worthy to live then; and of all, most unworthy of the great mercies I have had from God, who hath ever yet given me a heart which never yet feared foreign or home enemy. I speak it to give God the praise, as a testimony before you, and not to attribute anything to myself. For I, O Lord, what am I, whom practices and perils past should not fear? Or, what can I do? [*These words she spake with a great emphasis*] That I should speak for any glory, God forbid.

This, Mr. Speaker, I pray you deliver to the House, to whom heartily commend me. And so, I commit you all to your best fortunes and further counsels. And I pray you, Mr. Comptroller, Mr. Secretary, and you of my council, that before these gentlemen depart into their countries, you bring them all to kiss my hand.

THE QUEEN'S CORRESPONDENCE

The quality of Elizabeth's mind, her compassion, artistry and her stern views on kingship, religion and obedience are revealed in the following letters dictated but, except for an occasional postscript, never actually penned by the Queen. The selections fall into four groups: a letter to Queen Mary when Elizabeth was twenty-one and faced the very real possibility that her sister would order her execution; Elizabeth's correspondence with the crowned heads of Europe—Mary of Scotland, James VI of Scotland, and Catherine de Medici, Queen Regent of France; her letters to her military men and "beardless boys"; and finally, a few examples of her more intimate style of sympathy and encouragement to her friends, servants, and subjects.

To her sister, Mary Tudor, Queen of England
March 16, 1554

Elizabeth had been ordered to the Tower on suspicion that she had been involved in a plot to overthrow her sister.

IF ANY EVER did try this old saying "that a king's word was more than another man's oath," I most humbly beseech your Majesty to verify it to me, and to remember your last promise and my last demand, that I be not condemned without answer and due proof, which it seems that I now am, for that without cause proved, I am by your Council from you commanded to go to the Tower, a place more wanted for a false traitor than a true subject, which though I know I desire it not, yet in the face of all this realm it appears proved. I pray to God I may die the shamefullest death that any ever died, afore I may mean any such thing; and to this present hour I protest before God (Who shall judge my truth, whatsoever malice shall devise), that I never practised, counselled, nor consented to anything that might be prejudicial to your person anyway, or dangerous to the state by any means. And therefore I humbly beseech your Majesty to let me answer afore yourself, and not suffer me to trust to your Councillors, yea, and that afore I go to the Tower, if it be possible; if not, afore I be further condemned. Howbeit, I trust assuredly your Highness will give me leave to do it afore I go, that thus shamefully I may not be cried out on, as I now shall be; yea, and that without cause. Let conscience move your Highness to take some better way with me than to make me be condemned in all men's sight afore

From Henry Ellis, *Original Letters Illustrative of English History*, 2nd series (London, 1827), Vol. II, pp. 255-257.

may desert [be] known. Also I most humbly beseech your Highness to pardon this my boldness, which innocency procures me to do together with hope of your natural kindness, which I trust will not see me cast away without desert, which what it is I would desire no more of God but that you truly knew. Which thing I think and believe you shall never by report know, unless by yourself you hear. I have heard in my time of many cast away for want of coming to the presence of their Prince: and in late days I heard my Lord of Somerset say that if his brother had been suffered to speak with him he had never suffered; but the persuasions were made to him so great that he was brought in belief that he could not live safely if the Admiral lived, and that made him give consent to his death. Though these persons are not to be compared to your Majesty, yet I pray God, as evil persuasions persuade not one sister against the other, and all for that they have heard false report, and not hearken to the truth known. Therefore, once again, kneeling with humbleness of heart, because I am not suffered to bow the knees of my body, I humbly crave to speak with your Highness, which I would not be so bold as to desire if I knew not myself most clear, as I know myself most true. And as for the traitor Wyatt, he might peradventure write me a letter, but on my faith I never received any from him. And as for the copy of the letter sent to the French King, I pray God confound me eternally if ever I sent him word, message, token, or letter, by any means, and to this my truth I will stand in to my death.

Your Highness's most faithful subject, that hath been from the beginning, and will be to my end,

ELIZABETH

I humbly crave but only one word of answer from yourself.

To Mary Queen of Scots, June 23, 1567

Elizabeth had just learned that the Scottish nobility had rebelled against Mary, who had married James Hepburn, Earl of Bothwell, after the murder of her husband Lord Darnley. Darnley was as closely related to Elizabeth as Mary since both were descended, by different marriages, from Elizabeth's aunt, Margaret Tudor.

MADAM, It has been always held for a special principal in friendship that prosperity provideth but adversity proveth friends, whereof at this time finding occasion to verify the same in our actions, we have thought well both for our profession and your comfort in these few words to testify our friendship....

We have understood by your trusty servant, Robert Melville, such things as you gave him in charge to declare on your behalf concerning your estate and specially of as much as could be said for and allowed of your marriage. Madam, to be plain with you, our grief hath not been small that in this your marriage no

From G.B. Harrison, *The Letters of Queen Elizabeth I* (London: Cassell and Co., Ltd., 1935, 1968), Letter XVI, pp. 50-51. Reprinted by permission of the author.

slender consideration has been had that, as we perceive manifestly no good friend you have in the whole world can like thereof, and, if we should otherwise write or say, we should abuse you. For how could a worse choice be made for your honour than in such haste to marry such a subject who, besides other notorious lacks, public fame has charged with the murder of your late husband, besides the touching of yourself in some part, though we trust in that behalf falsely. And with what peril have you married him, that hath another lawful wife alive, whereby neither by God's law nor man's yourself can be his lawful wife nor any children betwixt you legitimate? Thus you see plainly what we think of the marriage; we are heartily sorry that we can conceive no better, what colourable reasons soever we have heard of your servant to induce us therein. Whereof we wish upon the death of your husband that first care had been to have searched out and punished the murderers of our near cousin, your husband, which having been done effectually, as easily it might have been in a matter so notorious, there might have been many more things tolerated better in your marriage than now can be suffered to be spoken of, and surely we cannot but for friendship to yourself besides the natural instinction that we have of blood to your late husband, profess ourselves earnestly bent to do anything in our power to prevent the due punishment of that murder against any subject you have, how dear soever you should hold him, and next thereto, to be careful how your son, the Prince, may be preserved to the comfort of you and your Realm. Which two things we have from the beginning always taken to heart, and herein do mean to continue, and would be very sorry but you should allow us therein, what dangerous persuasions soever be made to you for the contrary. Now for your comfort in such adversity...having a great part of your nobility, as we hear, separated from you, we assure you that whatsoever we can imagine meet for your honour and surety that shall lie in our power, we will perform the same that it shall and will appear you have a good neighbour, a dear sister and a faithful friend, and so shall you undoubtedly always find and prove us to be..., for which purpose we are determined to send with all speed one of our own trusty servants, not only to understand your state but also thereupon so to deal with your nobility and people as they shall find you not to lack our friendship and power for the preservation of your honour in quietness. And upon knowledge had what shall be further right to be done for your comfort and for the tranquillity of your Realm we will omit no time to further the same as you shall and will see, and so we recommend ourselves to you good sister in as effectual a manner as heretofore we were accustomed.

To Catherine de Medici, Queen Regent of France, October 16, 1567

Catherine had written on behalf of Mary of Scotland, who had been imprisoned by her rebellious subjects. The King referred to by Elizabeth was Catherine's son, Charles IX.

From Agnes Strickland, *Lives of the Queens of England* (London, 1851-1852), Vol. IV, p. 268.

HAVING learned by your letter, Madame, of which Monsieur Pasquier is the bearer, your honourable intention, and that of the King, my brother, on the part of my desolate cousin the Queen of Scots, I rejoice me very much to see that one Prince takes to heart the wrongs done to another, having a hatred to that metamorphosis, where the head is removed to the foot, and the heels hold the highest place. I promise you, Madame, that even if my consanguinity did not constrain me to wish her all honour, her example would seem too terrible for neighbours to behold, and for all Princes to hear. These evils often resemble the noxious influence of some baleful planet, which, commencing in one place, without the good power, might well fall in another, not that (God be thanked) I have any doubts on my part, wishing that neither the King my good brother, nor any other Prince, had more cause to chastise their bad sub-jects than I have to avenge myself on mine, which are always as faithful to me as I could desire; notwithstanding which, I never fail to condole with those Princes who have cause to be angry. Even those troubles that formerly began with the King have vexed me before now. Monsieur Pasquier (as I believe) thinks I have no French, by the passions of laughter into which he throws me by the formal precision with which he speaks and expresses himself.

Beseeching you, Madame, if I can at this time do you any pleasure, you will let me know, that I may acquit myself as a good friend on your part. In the meantime, I cannot cease to pray the Creator to guard the King and yourself from your bad subjects, and to have you always in His holy care.

In haste, at Hampton Court this 16th of October.

Your good sister and cousin,
ELIZABETH

To James VI of Scotland, July 6, 1590

Elizabeth had been having trouble with the Puritans at home and took this occasion to lecture James on the subject.

GREATER promises, more affection, and grants of more acknowledgings of received good turns, my dear Brother, none can better remember than this gentleman by your charge hath made me understand; whereby I think all my endeavours well recompensed, that see them so well acknowledged; and do trust that my counsels, if they so much content you, will serve for memorials to turn your actions to serve the turn of your safe government, and make the lookers-on honour your worth, and reverence such a ruler.

And lest fair semblance, that easily may beguile, do not breed your ignorance of such persons as either pretend religion or dissemble devotion, let me warn you that there is risen, both in your Realm and mine, a sect of perilous conse-

From John Bruce, *Letters of Queen Elizabeth and King James VI of Scotland,* original series (London: Camden Society, 1849), Vol. XLVI, p. 63.

quence, such as would have no Kings but a presbytery, and take our place while they enjoy our privilege, with a shade of God's Word, which none is judged to follow right without by their censure they be so deemed. Yea, look we well unto them. When they have made in our people's hearts a doubt of our religion, and that we err if they say so, what perilous issue this may make I rather think than mind to write....I pray you stop the mouths, or make shorter the tongues, of such ministers as dare presume to make orison [a prayer] in their pulpits for the persecuted in England for the Gospel.

Suppose you, my dear Brother, that I can tolerate such scandals of my sincere government? No. I hope, howsoever you be pleased to bear with their audacity towards yourself, yet you will not suffer a strange King receive that indignity at such caterpillars' hand, that instead of fruit, I am afraid will stuff your Realm with venom. Of this I have particularized more to this bearer, together with other answers to his charge, beseeching you to hear them, and not to give more harbour-room to vagabond traitors and seditious inventors, but to return them to me, or banish them your land. And thus, with my many thanks for your honorable entertainment of my late embassade, I commit you to God, Who ever preserve you from all evil counsel, and send you grace to follow the best.

Your most assured loving sister and cousin,

ELIZABETH R.

To James VI of Scotland, September 11, 1592

James had been having trouble with the nobility, who were up in arms against him, forcing James to make concessions to them.

The Dear care, my Brother, that ever I carried, from your infancy of your prosperous estate and quiet, could not permit hear of so many, yea so traitorous attempts, without unspeakable dolour and unexpressful woe....To redouble crimes so oft, I say with your pardon, must to your charge, which never durst have been renewed if the first had received the condign [deserving] reward; for slacking of due correction engenders the bold minds for new crimes. And if my counsels had as well been followed as they were truly meant, your subjects had now better known their King, and you no more need of further justice. You find by sour experience what this neglect hath bred you.

I hear of so uncouth a way taken by some of your conventions, yea, agreed to by yourself, that I must [wonder] how you will be clerk to such lessons. Must a king be prescribed what councillors he will take as if you were their ward? Shall you be obliged to tie or undo what they list make or revoke? O Lord, what strange dreams hear I, that would God they were so, for then at my waking I

From John Bruce, *Letters of Queen Elizabeth and King James VI of Scotland*, Vol. XLVI, pp. 75-76.

should find them fables. If you mean, therefore, to reign, I exhort you to show you worthy the place, which never can be surely settled without a steady course held to make you loved and feared. I assure myself many have escaped your hands more for dread of your remissness than for love of the escaped; so oft they see you cherishing some men for open crimes, and so they mistrust more their revenge than your assurance. My affection for you best lies on this, my plainness, whose patience is too much moved with these like everlasting faults.

And since it so likes you to demand my counsel, I find so many ways your state so unjointed, that it needs a skilfuller bonesetter than I to join each part in his right place. But to fulfill your will, take, in short, these few words: For all whoso you know the assailers of your courts, the shameful attempters of your sacred decree, if ever you pardon, I will never be the suitor. Who to peril a king were inventors or actors, they should crack a halter. Such is my charity. Who under pretence of bettering your estate, endangers the king, or needs will be his schoolmasters, if I might appoint their university they should be assigned to learn first to obey; so should they better teach you next. I am not so unskilful of a kingly rule that I would wink at no fault, yet would be open-eyed at public indignity. Neither should all have the whip though some were scourged. But if, like a toy, of a king's life so oft endangered nought shall follow but a scorn, what sequel I may doubt of such contempt I dread to think and dare not name. The rest I bequeath to the trust of your faithful servant, and pray the Almighty God to inspire you in time, afore too late, to cut their combs whose crest may danger you. I am void of malice, God is judge. I know them not. Forgive this too long a writing.

To Sir Thomas Heneage, February 10, 1586

The next three letters involve Robert Dudley, Earl of Leicester's actions in the Lowlands. The Earl was in command of the English army sent to help the rebellious Dutch provinces against the Spanish. Leicester was invited by the Dutch to become the supreme commander of all their forces; he accepted but neglected to ask the Queen's permission. Elizabeth was outraged and sent Thomas Heneage to the Lowlands with very precise instructions to Leicester.

YOU SHALL let the Earl understand how highly upon just cause we are offended with his late acceptation of the government of those provinces, being done contrary to our commandment delivered unto him both by ourself in speech and by particular letters from certain of our Council written unto him in that behalf by our express direction, which we do repute to be a very

From John Bruce, *Correspondence of Robert Dudley, Earl of Leicester during His Government of the Lowlands*, original series (London: Camden Society, 1844), Vol. XXVII, pp. 105-109.

great and strange contempt, least looked for at his hands, being he is a creature of our own; wherewith we have so much the greater cause to be offended, for that he hath not had that regard that became him....

You shall let him understand that we hold our honour greatly touched by the said acceptation of that government, and least as we may not with our honour endure, for that it carrieth a manifest appearance of repugnancy to our protestation set out in print by the which we declare that our only intent in sending him over into those parts was to direct and govern the English troops that we had granted to the States for their aid, and to assist them with his advice and counsel for the better ordering both of their civil and martial causes, as is contained in the late contract passed between us and their Commissioners that were here, so as the world may justly thereby conceive.

You shall say unto him that men of judgment will conceive another course taken by him; that the declaration published by us was but to abuse the world, for that they cannot in reason persuade themselves that a creature of our own, having for that purpose given him express commandmant, upon pain of his allegiance, to proceed, all delays and excuses laid apart, to the present demission thereof, considering the great obedience that even from the beginning of our reign hath been generally yielded us by our subjects, would ever have presumed to have accepted of the said government contrary to our commandment, without some secret assent of ours; or at least they will think that there is not now that reverent regard carried to our commandment as [hereto] for hath been, and as in the course of obedience ought to be.

For the removing of which hard conceit that the world may justly take, upon consideration either of the said abuse or contempt, you shall let him understand that our express pleasure and commandment is, upon pain of his allegiancy, that all delays and excuses set apart, without attending any further assembly of the States than such as shall be provided present with him at the time of your access there, or in some convenient place, he shall make an open and public resignation in the place where he accepted the same absolute government, as a thing done without our privity and consent contrary to the contract passed between us and their commissioners....

After the delivery of which message to the Earl, we think meet, to the end the States, or such as shall assist the Earl at the time of your arrival, may know the cause that moveth us to dislike of the said acceptance and to have the same revoked, that you shall advertise yourself to them and let them understand that we find it strange that a nobleman, a minister [of] ours, sent thither to execute and hold such a course of government as was contained in the said contract, should without our assent, be pressed to assent to accept of more large and absolute authority over the said countries than was accorded on by virtue of the said contract....

You shall further let them understand that forasmuch as we conceive that the said acceptation hath greatly wounded our honour, for the causes above specified, we have resolved to have the said Earl's authority revoked, requiring them therefore in our name to see the same executed out of hand....

To Robert Dudley, Earl of Leicester*
February 10, 1586

Heneage also took Leicester a personal blast from the Queen.

How contemptuously we conceive ourself to have been used by you, you shall by this bearer understand, whom we have expressly sent unto you to charge you withal. We could never have imagined had we not seen it fall out in experience that a man raised up by ourself and extraordinarily favoured by us above any other subject of this land, would have in so contemptible a sort broken our commandment, in a cause that so greatly toucheth us in honour; whereof, although you have showed yourself to make but little account in most undutiful a sort, you may not therefore think that we have so little care of the reparation thereof as we mind to pass so great a wrong in silence unredressed: and, therefore, our express pleasure and commandment is, that all delays and excuses laid apart, you do presently, upon the duty of your allegiance, obey and fulfill whatsoever the bearer hereof shall direct you to do in our name. Whereof fail you not, as you will answer the contrary at your uttermost peril.

To Sir Thomas Heneage,**
April 27, 1586

Heneage made the mistake of not following the Queen's instructions to the letter and took it upon himself to assure the Dutch that the Queen's anger in no way meant that she was either planning to pull out her army or to contemplate peace with the Spanish.

WHAT phlegmatical reasons soever were made you; how happened it that you will not remember that when a man hath faulted and committed by abettors thereto that neither the one nor the other will willingly make their own retreat. Jesus, what availeth wit when it fails the owner at greatest need? Do that you are bidden, and leave your considerations for your own affairs; for in some things you had clear commandment, which you did not; and in other none, and did. Yea, to the use of those speeches from me that might oblige me to more than I was bound or mind ever to yield. We Princes be wary enough of our bargains. Think you I will be bound by your speech to make no peace for mine own matters without their consent? It is enough that I injure not their country, nor themselves, in making peace for them, without their consent. I am assured of your dutiful thought, but I am utterly at squares with this childish dealing.

*From John Bruce, *Correspondence of Robert Dudley...*, Vol. XXVII, p. 110.
**Ibid.*, Vol. XXVII, p. 243.

To Robert Dudley, Earl of Leicester
July 18, 1586

Two months later the storm was over and Leicester had been forgiven, and Elizabeth was again using her term of endearment for Dudley—her "eyes."

ROB, I AM afraid you will suppose by my wandering writings that a mid-summer moon hath taken large possession of my brains this month, but you must needs take things as they come in my head, though order be left behind me. When I remember your request to have a discreet and honest man that may carry my mind and see how all goes there, I have chosen this bearer, whom you know and have made good trial of. I have fraught him full of my conceits of those country matters, and imparted what way I mind to take, and what is fit for you to use. I am sure you can credit him, and so I will be short with these few notes....And for Norris and other captains that voluntarily without commandment have many years ventured their lives and won our nation honour and themselves fame, [let them] be not discouraged by any means, neither by new-come men nor by old trained soldiers elsewhere. If there be fault in using of soldiers or making of profit by them, let them hear of it without open shame and doubt not but I will chasten them therefore. It frets me not a little that the poor soldier that hourly ventures life should want their due, that well deserve rather reward; and look in whom the fault may duly be proved, let them smart therefore. And if the Treasurer be found untrue or negligent, according to desert he shall be used; though you know my old wont, that love not to discharge from office without desert; God forbid. I pray you let this bearer know what may be learned herein; and for this treasure I have joined Sir Thomas Shirley to see all this money discharged in due sort where it needeth and behoveth. Now will I end that do imagine I talk still with you, and therefore loathly say farewell, ŏŏ, [Elizabeth's private code for the Earl's two eyes], though ever I pray God bless you from all harm and save you from all foes with my million and legion of thanks for all your pains and cares. As you know, ever the same.

E.R.

From G. B. Harrison, *The Letters of Queen Elizabeth I*, Letter VI, pp. 178-179. Reprinted by permission of the author.

To Robert Devereux, Earl of Essex*
April 15, 1589

Essex was the Queen's special favorite during the final years of
her life, as Dudley had been during the earlier decades. The Earl was
young and unruly, and skipped court to join Drake and Norris in
their attack on the Spanish treasure fleet.

ESSEX, Your sudden and undutiful departure from our presence and your place of attendance, you may easily conceive how offensive it is, and ought to be, unto us. Our great favours, bestowed on you without deserts, hath drawn you thus to neglect and forget your duty; for other constructions we cannot make of those your strange actions. Not meaning, therefore, to tolerate this your disordered part, we gave directions to some of our Privy Council to let you know our express pleasure for your immediate repair hither; which you have not performed, as your duty doth bind you, increasing greatly thereby your former offence and undutiful behaviour, in departing in such sort without our privity, having so special office of attendance and charge near our person. We do therefore charge and command you forthwith, upon receipt of these our letters, all excuses and delays set apart, to make your present and immediate repair unto us, to understand our further pleasure. Whereof see you fail not, as you will be loath to incur our indignation, and will answer for the contrary at your uttermost peril.

To Sir John Norris and Sir Francis Drake,**
May 4, 1589

Sir Roger Williams used his authority to convey Essex on board
the *Swiftsure* to the English fleet under Norris and Drake. Despite
the Queen's words Williams did not remain in Elizabeth's bad graces
for long.

TRUSTY and well beloved, we greet you well. Although we doubt not but of yourselves you have so thoroughly weighed the heinousness of the offence lately committed by Sir Roger Williams, that you have both discharged him from the place and charge which was appointed him in that army, and committed the same to some other meet person (as we doubt not but you have

---

*From Walter B. Devereux, *Lives and Letters of the Devereux, Earls of Essex in the Reigns of Elizabeth, James I, and Charles I, 1540-1646* (London, 1853), Vol. I, pp. 204-205.
**Ibid.*, Vol. I, pp. 199-201.

choice of as sufficient as he is), and that you have also laid punishment upon him according to his desert; yet we would not but you should also know from ourself, by these our special letters, our just wrath and indignation against him and lay before you his intolerable contempt against ourself, and the authority you have from us, in that he forsook the army, and conveyed away also one of our principal ships from the rest of the fleet. In which points his offence is in so high a degree, that the same deserveth by all laws to be punished by death, which if you have not already done (and whereunto we know your authority as General doth warrant you) then we will and command you that you sequester him from all charge and service, and cause him to be safely kept, so as he slip not away until you shall know our further pleasure therein, as you will answer to the contrary at your perils. For as we have authority to rule, so we look to be obeyed, and to have obedience directly and surely continued unto us, and so look to be answered herein at your hands. Otherwise we will think you unworthy of the authority you have, and that you know not how to use it. In the meantime we have also found it strange, that, before your departing from Plymouth, you should either be so careless, or suffer yourselves so easily to be abused, that any of our ships, much more a principal ship, should be in such manner conveyed away from the rest of the fleet, and afterwards, also being so near as Falmouth (as we understood) should not be your commandment and direction be stayed; a matter which we cannot but remember unto you, and yet we do hope that you are no partakers of the offence that is committed

And if Essex be now come into the company of the fleet, we straightly charge you that, all dilatory excuse set apart, you do forthwith cause him to be sent back hither in safe manner: which if you do not, you shall look to answer for the same to your smart, for these be no childish actions, nor matters wherein you are to deal by cunning of devises, to seek evasions, as the customs of lawyers is; neither will we be so satisfied at your hands. Therefore consider well of your doings herein.

To Robert Devereux, Earl of Essex
September 14, 1599

Essex had been sent in command of an English army to Ireland to subdue the extensive and serious rebellion of the Earl of Tyrone. Essex botched the job, and the Queen wrote the following letter.

RIGHT TRUSTY and well beloved cousin...we greet you well. Having sufficiently declared unto you before this time how little the manner of your proceedings hath answered either our direction or the world's expectation, and finding now by your letters by Cuffe [the Earl's secretary] a course more strange, if strange may be, we are doubtful what to prescribe you at any time, or

From Walter B. Devereux, *Lives and Letters of the Devereux*, Vol. II, pp. 61-65, and from G. B. Harrison, *The Letters of Queen Elizabeth I*, pp. 270-273.

what to build upon your writing unto us in anything. For we have clearly discerned of late, what you have ever to this hour possessed us with expectation, that you would proceed as we have directed you; but your actions always show the contrary, though carried in such sort, as we were sure to have no time to countermand them. Before your departure, no man's counsel was held sound, which persuaded not presently the main prosecution in Ulster; all was nothing without that; and nothing was too much for that. This drew on the sudden transportation of so many thousands, to be carried over with you; and, when you arrived, we were charged with more than the list on which we resolved, by the number of 300 horsemen above the thousand, which was assented to, which were only to be in pay during service in Ulster. We have been also put in charge ever since the first journey, the pretence of which voyage, [as] appeared by your letters, was to do some present service in the interim, while that grew more commodious the main prosecution. For which purpose you did importune with great earnestness that all manner of provisions might be hastened to Dublin against your return. Of this resolution to defer your going into Ulster you may well think that we would have made stay, if you had given us more time by warning....Then we received another letter of new reasons to suspend that journey yet awhile, to draw the army into Offally, the fruit whereof at your homecoming was nothing else but new relations of further missing of our army, and greater difficulties to perform the Ulster wars. Then followed from you and the Council a new demand of two thousand men, to which if we would assent, you would speedily undertake what we had so often commanded. When that was granted, and your going onward promised by divers letters, we received by this bearer new fresh advertisement, that all you can do is to go to the frontiers, and that you have provided only twenty days' victuals. In which kind of proceeding we must deal plainly with you....Whosoever shall examine any of the arguments used for excuse, shall find your own proceedings beget the difficulties, and that no just causes do breed the alterations of lack of numbers. If sickness of the army be the reason, why was there not the action undertaken when the army was in better state? If winter's approach, why were the summer months of July and August lost? If the spring were too soon, and the summer that followed otherwise spent, if the harvest that succeeded were so neglected as nothing hath been done, then surely we must conclude that none of the four quarters of the year will be in season for you and that Council to agree of Tyrone's persecution, for which all our charge is intended. Further we require you to consider whether we have not a great cause to think that your purpose is not to end the war, when you yourself have often told us that all the petty undertakings in Leix, Munster and Connaught, are but loss of time, consumption of treasure, and, most of all, our people, until Tyrone himself be first beaten, on whom all the rest depend....

How often have you told us that others, that preceded you, had no judgment to end the war, who often resolved [explained to] us [that], until Lough Foyle and Ballyshannon were planted, there could be no hope of doing service upon the capital rebels? We must therefore let you know, as it cannot be ignorance, so it cannot be want of means; for you had our asking, you had choice of times, you had power and authority more ample than ever any had, or ever shall have. It may well be judged with how little contentment we seek this and other errors. But how should that be hid which is so palpable?...

To conclude, if you say that our army be in a list nineteen thousand, [and] that you have them not, we answer then to you, our Treasurer, that we are evil served, and that there needs not so frequent demands of full pay. If you will say that the muster master is to blame, we must muse then, why he is not punished....For the small proportion you say you carry with you of 3,500 foot, when lately we augmented you 2000 more, it is past comprehension, except it be that you have left too great numbers in unnecessary garrisons, which do increase our charge, and diminish our army, which we command you to reform, especially since, by your continual report of the state of every province, you describe them to be in worse conditions than ever they were before you put foot in that kingdom....And therefore because we see now, by your own word, that the hope is spent of this year's service upon Tyrone and O'Donnell, we do command you and our Council to fall jointly into present deliberation of the state which

you have brought our kingdom unto; and...secondly, we look to hear from you and them jointly, how you think fit that the remain of this year shall be spent and employed, in what kind of war, and whose, and with what numbers; which being done and sent hither in writing with all expedition, you shall then understand our pleasure in all things fit for your service; until which time we command you to be very careful to meet with all inconveniences that may rise in the kingdom, where the evil-affected will grow so insolent upon our evil success, and the good subjects grow desperate, when they see the best of our defending them....

And thus, expecting your answer, we end, at our manor of Nonsuch, the 14th of September, 1599.

To Lady Paget, undated*
(on the death of Lady Paget's daughter)

CALL TO MIND, good Kate, how hardly we princes can brook [the] crossing of our commands; how ireful will the Highest Power be (may you be sure) when murmurings shall be made

of his pleasingest will? Let nature therefore not hurt herself, but give place to the giver. Though this lesson be from a silly vicar, yet it is sent from a loving sovereign.

To Henry Carey, Lord Hunsdon**
February 26, 1570

Hunsdon had won a decisive victory over Leonard Darce during the Rebellion of the North in the winter of 1569-1570.

WE ARE right glad that it hath pleased God to assist you in your late service against that cankered subtle traitor, Leonard Darce, whose force being far greater in number than

yours, you have overthrown, and he thereupon was the first that fled, having a heart readier to show his unloyal falsehood than to abide the fight; though we could have desired to have him taken,

*From Agnes Strickland, *Lives of the Queens of England*, Vol. IV, p. 429.
**From *Calendar of State Papers Domestic: Addenda. Series of the Reign of Elizabeth*, ed. Mary Green (London, 1871), pp. 245-246.

yet we thank God that he is overthrown, and forced to fly our Realm to his like company of rebels, whom we doubt not but God will confound with such ends as are meet for them.

We will not now by words express how inwardly glad we are that you have had such success, whereby your courage in such an unequal match, your faithfulness and your wisdom is seen to the world, this being the first fight in field in our time against rebels; but we mean also by just reward to let the world see how much we esteem such a service as this is, and we would have you thank God heartily, and comfort yourself with the assurance of our favour. We have also sent our letter of thanks to Sir John Forster, and would have you thank our faithful sol-

diers of Berwick, in whose service we repose no small trust.

[To which the Queen added in her own hand:]

I doubt much, my Harry, whether that the victory were given me more joyed me, or that you were by God appointed the instrument of my glory; and I assure you for my country's good, the first might suffice, but for my heart's contentation, the second more pleased me. It likes me not a little that, with a good testimony of your faith, there is seen a stout courage of your mind, that more trusted to the goodness of your quarrel than to the weakness of your number.

Your loving kinswoman,
Elizabeth R.

To George Talbot, Earl of Shrewsbury
October 21, 1562

Elizabeth had been seriously ill and Shrewsbury had written a get-well note, to which the Queen responded.

Right trusty and right well-beloved cousin and councillor, we greet you well. By your letters sent to us we perceive that you have heard of some late sickness wherewith we were visited; whereof as you had cause to be greatly grieved, so, though you heard of our amendment, and was thereby recomforted, yet, for a satisfaction of your mind, you are desirous to have the state of our amendment certified by some few words in a letter from ourself. True it is that we were about thirteen days past distempered as commonly happeneth in the beginning of a fever, but after two or

three days, without any great inward sickness, there began to appear certain red spots in some part of our face, likely to prove the smallpox; but, thanked be God, contrary to the expectation of our physicians, and all others about us, the same so vanished away as within four or five days passed no token almost appeared; and at this day, we thank God, we are so free from any token or mark of any such disease that none can conjecture any such thing. So as by this you may perceive what was our sickness, and in what good estate we be; thanking you, good cousin, for the care you had of the

From E. Lodge, *Illustrations of British History* (London, 1791), Vol. II, p. 79. Lodge has misdated this letter by ten years.

one, and of the comfort you take of the other, wherein we do assure ourself of as much fidelity, duty and love, you bear us as of any, of any degree within our realm. Given at our Castle of Windsor, the 22nd of October, 1562, the 4th year of our Reign.

[*To which the Queen added in her own hand*]

MY FAITHFUL SHREWSBURY,

Let no grief touch your heart for fear of my disease; for I assure you, if my credit were not greater than my show, there is no beholder would believe that ever I had been touched with such a malady.

Your faithful, loving Sovereign,
ELIZABETH R.

To John Harington,*
March, 1575

Harington, a boy of fourteen, was the Queen's godson. She sent him a copy of her speech to Parliament given on the 15th of the month.

BOY JACK, I have made a clerk write fair my poor words for thine use, as it cannot be such striplings have entrance into Parliament assembly as yet. Ponder them in thy hours of leisure, and play with them till they enter thine understanding; so shalt thou hereafter, perchance, find some good fruits hereof when thy Godmother is out of remembrance; and I do this because thy father was ready to serve and love us in trouble and thrall.

To Walter Devereux, Earl of Essex**
August 6, 1575

Walter Devereux was the father of Robert, whose letters from the Queen have already been cited. Walter had been campaigning in Ireland; in her own hand the Queen added the following postscript to the official letter of thanks.

IF LINES could value life, or thanks could answer praise, I should esteem my pen's labour the best employed time that many years hath lent me. But to supply the want that both these carrieth, a right judgment of upright dealing shall lengthen the scarcity that either of the other wanted. Deem, therefore, Cousin mine, that the search of your honour, with the danger of your breath, hath not been bestowed on so ungrateful a Prince that will not both consider the one and reward the other.

Your most loving cousin and Sovereign,

E.R.

*From John Harington, *Nugae Antiquae*, ed. T. Park (London, 1804), Vol. I, p. 127.
**From Walter B. Devereux, *Lives and Letters of the Devereux*, Vol. I, p. 119.

To George Talbot, Earl of Shrewsbury
September 5, 1582

(on the death of his son)

WE HAD thought immediately upon understanding of the death of the Lord Talbot your son, to have sent you our letters of comfort, but that we were loath that they should have been the first messengers unto you of so unpleasant matter as the loss of a son of so great hope and towardness, that might have served to have been a comfortable staff unto you in your old years, and a profitable pillar unto this our estate in time to come, whereof he gave as great hope as any one of his calling within this our Realm; which we know, in respect of the love you bear us, cannot but greatly increase your grief. But herein, we, as his Prince and Sovereign, and you as a loving and natural father, for that we both be interested in the loss (though for several respects), are to lay aside our particular causes of grief, and to remember that God, Who hath been the worker thereof, and doeth all things for the best, is not to be controlled. Besides, if we do duly look into the matter in true course of Christianity, we shall then see that the loss hath wrought so great a gain to the gentleman whom we now lack, as we have rather cause to rejoice than lament; for if the imperfections of this declining age we live in be truly weighed, and the sundry miseries that we are daily subject unto be duly looked into, we shall then find more cause to judge them unhappy that live, than to bewail those as unfortunate that are dead. But, for that the weakness of frail flesh cannot so rest upon that comfort which the happy estate of his change hath wrought but that nature will have her force, we cannot therefore but put you in mind how well God in His singular goodness hath dealt with you, in that He left you behind other sons of great hope, who through the good education that you have carefully given them, and the good gifts of nature they are plentifully endowed withal, are like to prove no less comfortable unto you than serviceable unto us. And, therefore, for your comfort you are to remember that, of four sons that He hath given you, He hath taken only one to Himself. These reasons, which we have thought on and used with good fruit as seems to lessen our own grief, we have thought meet to impart them unto you, and do hope they shall work no less effect in you, whose case we tender as much as our own, having made as great trial of your care and fidelity towards us as ever Prince hath made of servant. And, therefore, we do assure ourself that in this discomfort there is no earthly thing can yield you more comfort than the assurance of our gracious favour towards you; whereof you may make full account to receive the same from us in as full measure as a well-deserving servant and subject may in true gratuity look for at a gracious and thankful Prince's hands.

From G.B. Harrison, *The Letters of Queen Elizabeth I*, Letter XXXV, pp. 157-158. Reprinted by permission of the author.

To William Cecil, Lord Burghley*
May 8, 1583

Burghley was the Queen's chief minister. Despondent and over-worked, he was threatening to resign.

SIR SPIRIT, I doubt I do nickname you for those of your kind, they say, have no sense. But I have lately seen an *ecce signum*, that if an ass kick you, you feel it too soon. I will recant you from being spirit, if ever I perceive that you disdain not such a feeling. Serve God, fear the King, and be a good fellow to the rest. Let never care appear in you for such a rumour, but let them well know that you desire the righting of such wrong by making known their error, than you to be so silly a soul as to forshow what you ought to do, or not freely deliver what you think meetest, and pass of no man so much, as not to regard her trust who putteth it in you.

God bless you, and long may you last,

Omnino E.R.

THE QUEEN'S POEMS

Elizabeth's poem "On Monsieur's Departure" is reasonably well authenticated; presumably it was written in 1582. The Duke of Anjou returned to France without having persuaded the Queen to marry him. At forty-nine Elizabeth momentarily dropped the careful facade of majesty and spoke from the heart. The Queen's metric translation of Boethius' *Consolation of Philosophy* was written in 1593 and is reported to have been completed in a month. The selection is her rendering of the sixth verse of Book III.

On Monsieur's Departure**

I grieve and dare not show my discontent,
I love and yet am forced to seem to hate,
I do, yet dare not say I ever meant,
I seem stark mute but inwardly do prate.
  I am and not, I freeze and yet am burned,
  Since from myself another self I turned.

*From Agnes Strickland, *Lives of the Queens of England,* Vol. IV, p. 470.
**Reprinted from John Nichols, *Progresses of Queen Elizabeth* (London, 1823), Vol. II, p. 346.

My care is like my shadow in the sun,
Follows me flying, flies when I pursue it,
Stands and lies by me, doth what I have done.
His too familiar care doth make me rue it.
    No means I find to rid him from my breast,
    Till by the end of things it be supprest.

Some gentler passion slide into my mind,
For I am soft and made of melting snow;
Or be more cruel, love, and so be kind.
Let me or float or sink, be high or low.
    Or let me live with some more sweet content,
    Or die and so forget what love ere meant.

Boethius' Consolation of Philosophy

All human kind on earth
    From like beginning comes:
One father is of all,
    One only all doth guide.
He gave to sun the beams
    And horns on moon bestowed;
He men to earth did give
    And signs to heaven.
He closed in limbs our souls
    Fetched from highest seat.
A noble seed therefore brought forth
    All mortal folk.
What crake you of your stock
    Or forefathers old?
If your first spring and author
    God you view,
No man bastard be,
    Unless with vice the worst he feed
And leaveth so his birth.

Reprinted from *Queen Elizabeth's Englishings,* ed. Caroline Pemberton, original series 113 (London: Early English Text Society, 1899), p. 54.

III. ANOTHER PERSPECTIVE: WORKING WITH GLORIANA

The following letters involve two men who were extremely close to Elizabeth and knew her well. William Cecil was Gloriana's chief minister for about forty years, first as her Principal Secretary and later as Lord Treasurer. As Lord Burghley he was also one of the few commoners she ever elevated to the peerage. Robert Devereux, Earl of Essex was the Queen's flaming favorite during the autumn of her life. Generally she kept her court "favorites" and her state servants such as Cecil separate, but in the case of Essex she made an exception, for he joined the council in 1593. Essex proved to be a highly unstable young man, and his association with Elizabeth eventually destroyed him. After the disaster of his Irish campaign in 1599, he suffered something akin to a nervous breakdown, indulged in "suicidal" treason against the Queen and was executed in 1601.

The letters of Cecil and Essex reveal Elizabeth in a variety of guises, not all of them pleasant. Clearly, working with the Queen could be frustrating, humiliating, exhausting, and at times dangerous. The question remains: How did she get away with being so perverse—even nasty?

William Cecil to the Queen, December, 1560

Cecil and the majority of the Queen's council recommended an active, aggressive policy in Scotland, in aid of the Protestant faction and in opposition to the French-supported Catholic party. Elizabeth, however, did not approve of meddling in other princes' kingdoms and, much to Cecil's frustration, opposed his policy.

IT MAY please your most Excellent Majesty — With a sorrowful heart and watery eyes, I your poor servant and most lowly subject, an unworthy Secretary, beseech your Majesty to pardon this my lowly suit, that considering the proceeding in this matter for removing the French out of Scotland doth not content your Majesty, and that I cannot with my conscience give any contrary advice, I may, with your Majesty's favour and clemency, be spared to entermeddle therein. And this I am forced to do of necessity, for I will never be a minister in any your Majesty's service, whereunto your own mind shall not be agreeable, for thereunto I am sworn, to be a minister of your Majesty's determinations and not of mine own, or of others, though they be never so many. And on the other part to serve your Majesty in anything that myself cannot

From Thomas Wright, *Queen Elizabeth and Her Times* (London, 1838), Vol. I, pp. 24-25.

allow, must needs be an unprofitable service, and so untoward, as therein I would be loath your Majesty should be deceived. And as for any other service, though it were in your Majesty's kitchen or garden, from the bottom of my heart I am ready without respect of estimation, wealth or ease, to do your Majesty's commandment to my life's end. Whereof I wish with all my poor sorrowful heart, that your Majesty would make some proof, for this I do affirm, that I have not had since your Majesty's reign, any one day's joy, but in your Majesty's honour and weale.

William Cecil to Nicholas Throgmorton
August 20, 1567

Elizabeth was outraged that the Scottish nobility should have imprisoned their Queen and forced her to abdicate in favor of her year-old son, James I, with the Earl of Murray as regent. The following letter of instruction to Throgmorton, who was the Queen's ambassador in Edinburgh, was written with Elizabeth's anger as background. The italicized sentences were underlined by Cecil in the original letter.

THE VERY cause of staying still [in Scotland] is that her Majesty would have you expedite the proceeding of the Earl of Murray, as concerning the acceptation of her government. The Queen's Majesty is in a continual offence against all those Lords, and we here, that cannot move her Majesty to mitigate it, do what we can to move her to hide it more than she doth. But surely the more we deal in it the more danger some of us find of her indignation and specially in conceiving that we are not dutifully minded to her Majesty as our sovereign. *And where such thorns be it is no quiet treading.* For howsoever her Majesty shall in this cause touching her so nearly, as it seemeth she conceiveth, though I firmly trust without any instant cause, be offended with my argument I will, after my opinion declared, obey her Majesty to do that which is my office....

Very sorry I am to behold the likelihood of the loss of the fruits of seven or eight years negotiation with Scotland and now to suffer a divorce betwixt this realm and that, where neither of the countries shall take either good or pleasure thereof.

If religion may remain I trust the divorce shall be rather in words and terms than in hearts. And of this I have no great doubt, especially if my Lord of Murray shall take upon him the government.

After I had written this much I thought, before I would send away these letters, to move her Majesty what I should write to you concerning the allowance of any ambassador from that young King [James VI]. Wherein she so misliked my notice as she noted in me no small folly, adding that she would never admit anything in such sort prejudicial to

From Conyers Read, *Mr. Secretary Cecil and Queen Elizabeth* (New York: Alfred A. Knopf and Co., 1955), pp. 385-387. Reprinted by permission of the publisher.

the Queen [of Scotland] *until she were perfectly informed that she were therein contented....*

Secondly, I moved her to know what time you should depart thence, considering you have nothing further to deal, for-that with the Queen you could not treat and with the Lords her Majesty would not allow you to treat in affirmation of their authority, and without affirmation I did see they would not deal with you in any matter worth your tarrying.

After much speech her Majesty assented to these points following:

1. You should procure answer to her Majesty's earnest messages lately committed to your charge in favour of the Queen.

2. Next, you should once again attempt by means of the Lord of Murray to see the Queen.

3. Thirdly you should use all the means you could to induce my Lord of Murray to take or refuse the regency as he should find it most beneficial for the saving of the Queen's life.

And yet her Majesty would have you say in her name to the Earl of Murray that it will be a hard thing for him to avoid public ignominy of the world if he take upon him the regency; and that until her Majesty may certainly know that it is the Queen her sister's mind, without coercion, that he should be the governor, she will never admit anything that will affirm the same.

And in this sort her Majesty concluded, being again put in remembrance, that when you have executed these messages and found what the Earl of Murray would do for accepting or refusing the government, you might return home. And so she was content I should write as I do.

Now percase you will marvel that hereof you have not her Majesty's own letter—whereof one cause is for that presently her Majesty is troubled with a crick in her neck as by great pain thereof she can neither much attend affairs, nor yet sign any letters. Another cause is for your advantage, that percase her Majesty might find some cause to alter her mind upon a new motion....

Thus have I written at length, whilst others are here occupied with hunting at length. *God send me quietness at length or freedom from evil will shortly.*

William Cecil to Sir Francis Walsingham
June 5, 1571

The following letter gives a glimpse of the Queen's diplomatic style. Her council was trying to arrange a marriage between Elizabeth and the Duke of Anjou, brother to the King of France and, of course, a Catholic. The "articles" referred to are the terms of the proposed marriage treaty. Walsingham was, at the time, negotiating with the French in Paris. The French port of Calais had been in English hands for hundreds of years and was symbolic of England's past military greatness, but it had been lost in the disastrous war with France during Mary's reign. Elizabeth always wanted the city and was forever trying to devise some means—generally short of war—to get it back.

From Dudley Digges, *The Compleat Ambassador* (London, 1655), p. 104.

IR, YOU must bear with my slow dispatches in returning your servants, for that I cannot obtain such resolutions as may give cause to write, whereupon I am forced to bear here patiently the lack that I find, and you must do the like on your part, hoping that *Deus dabit meliora*. Now I send away this bearer, meaning and hoping to send herewith the great answer, and to give you some light hereof. Thus it is, the French ambassador upon the receipt of his last answers, agreeable with your letters, pressed the Queen's Majesty to have the rest of the articles on her part, which in no wise she would agree unto, pretending that without a resolute answer to the article of religion this could not be; wherewith the ambassador was so wounded as indeed in conference with him I found him desperate in the matter and entered into passions. But after some speech used with him I pacified him, with hope that the Q. Majesty might be by further persuasions induced to show the rest of the articles. And so with some long laborious persuasions her Majesty was induced to agree that the articles should be made ready and showed, as things earnestly pressed by that King and his ambassador here,
with which pretence her Majesty thought her honour saved well. Hereof I was appointed to inform the ambassador, and then was I also commanded to put the articles in readiness, which were not unready as I conceived. But ere I could finish them I was commanded to conclude them with a request to have Calais restored, a matter so inconvenient to bring forth a marriage as indeed I thought it meant to procure a breach. And so the matter continued in my opinion desperate, but with good help it was remedied. I desired that the Queen's Majesty would let my Lord Marquess, the Earls of Sussex and Leicester to see the articles, and so they did, and very honourably and wisely gave counsel to forbear that toy of Calais, and generally did further the prosecution of the marriage as a matter of all other most necessary at this time. And now we take it that her Majesty intendeth it earnestly, whereupon yesterday in the afternoon my Lord of Leicester and I have delivered unto the ambassador a copy of the articles, which at the first hearing he did not mislike. What he will do this day I know not, but certainly they are very reasonable....

Sir Thomas Smith to William Cecil
March, 1575

Cecil was away from court, and the job of "managing" the Queen fell to Smith, one of the two Principal Secretaries.

OR MATTERS of state I will write as soon as I can have any access to her Majesty, the which, as it was when your Lordship was here sometime so,
sometime no, and all times uncertain and ready to stays and revocation.... This irresolution doth weary and kill her ministers, destroy her actions and overcome

all good designs and counsels—no letters touching Ireland, although read and allowed by her Majesty, yet can I get signed. I wait whilst I neither have eyes to see or legs to stand upon. And yet these delays grieve me more and will not let me sleep in the night....For private matters and suits I have the same success. They increase daily. Yea nor nay can I get,...We need within a while to have a horse or an ass to carry bills after us, increasing daily and never dispatched.

William Cecil to Sir Christopher Hatton
March 15, 1587

Cecil describes his desperate predicament in the face of the Queen's wrath over his part in the execution of Mary Queen of Scots.

I AM SO wounded by the late sharp and most heavy speech of her Majesty to myself in the hearing of my Lord of Leicester and Mr. Secretary Walsingham, expressing therein her indignation at such time as I was called to her presence for matters of the Low Countries, myself giving no occasion by any speech of the matters of the Queen of Scots until her Majesty did charge me therewith; as since, regarding with myself the weight and nature of her Majesty's displeasure so settled and increased, and mine own humility, not able without my heart bleeding to abide the countenance of such her displeasure, I am most careful how by any means to me possible, I may shun all increase of this her Majesty's so weighty offence, knowing it very true that was said by the wise king, *Indignatio principis mors est*. And though my conscience doth witness me in the sight of God, to whose everlasting indignation and loss of my body and soul I commit myself if I say an untruth, I never had thought, nor did ever any act with thought to offend her Majesty. But now, finding this bitter burden of her Majesty's displeasure rather increased than diminished, since her Majesty, of her princely compassion, admitted me first to her service upon her late displeasure, I have cause to fear that this increase groweth more by means of some secret enemies than of any hard influence of her own princely nature.

And therefore, though I cannot imagine that any person is my enemy for any private offences committed...but only in respect of my service to her Majesty, wherein I know I have procured of long time many mislikings for doing my duty.

Yet, being so publicly known as I find it to be, that her Majesty is grievously offended against me, as my enemies presume her ears to be open to any calumniation to be devised against me.

Seeing I cannot devise any remedy against the malice of men that may be devised for things past, but only hope upon her Majesty's gracious interpreta-

From Conyers Read, *Lord Burghley and Queen Elizabeth*, pp. 374-375. Reprinted by permission of the publisher.

tion by experience of my service past, yet now, in this time of her Majesty's disfavour, whereof evil disposed persons may take advantage, for anything to be done by me presently, I think it needful for myself to life warily, and of duty to her Majesty to withdraw myself from all voluntary public actions of state whereunto I am not expressly by her Majesty commanded, until I may be relieved with such comfort to come to her presence as others have.

William Cecil to Robert Devereux, Earl of Essex
November 22, 1596

In the war with Spain the English expedition against Cadiz had been a spectacular but expensive success, and Elizabeth was determined to keep for her own coffers as much of the profits of war as possible.

MY LORD, My hand is weak, my mind troubled. And therefore my letter must be shorter than the subject offered me and a few lines be interpreted with favour until I may by speech add a commentary in paraphrase.

I came from Court with the burden of her Majesty's displeasure expressed, as my Lord Buckhurst and Sir John Fortescue did hear, with words of indignity, reproach, rejecting me as a miscreant and coward for that I would not assent unto her opinion that your Lordship ought [not] to have the profit of the prisoners, wishing her to hear you both with what conditions your Lordship received them...But herewith her Majesty increased her ireful speeches that I, either through fear or favour, regarded you more than herself, which she said she did otherwise observe in me. But hereof I have no comfort to write much now, being come thence laden with grief for her so implacable displeasure, only for this your cause.

I am further laden with report of your displeasure [against me]…. Her Majesty chargeth and condemneth me for favouring of you against her. Your Lordship, contrarywise, misliketh me for pleasing of her Majesty to offend you. My case is miserable if against you both I had not comfort by God through a good conscience,…Otherwise I see no possibility…to shun both these dangers but by obtaining of license to live an anchorite, or some such private life whereunto I am meetest, for my age, my infirmity and my daily decaying estate.

From Thomas Birch, *Memoirs of the Reign of Queen Elizabeth from the year 1581 till her death...* (London, 1754), Vol. II, p. 176.

Lord Admiral Charles Howard to William Cecil*
October 10, 1597

Cecil was old, sick and had only a year to live. He had written Elizabeth a thank-you note for having appointed his son Robert chancellor of the Duchy of Lancaster.

M Y HONORED Lord, your letter being delivered unto her Majesty, and having read it unto me, [she] commanded me to write this to your Lordship that you do not give her so many thanks for that she did to your son, as she giveth herself for the doing that which may any way comfort you, and also to give your lordship thanks from her for your kind and most thankful letter; and sayeth although you have brought up your son as near as may be like unto yourself for her service, yet are you to her in all things and shall be Alpha and Omega. Her Majesty also prayeth your Lordship that you will forbear the travail of your hand though she is sure you will not of your head for her service. Her Majesty giveth your son great thanks, that he was the cause of your stay, for she sayeth wheresoever your Lordship is, your service to her giveth hourly thanks; and prayeth your Lordship to use all the rest possible you may, that you may be able to serve her at this time that cometh. My honorable Lordship, let me crave pardon that for want of memory cannot so fully write her Majesty's gracious words and her thanks to your Lordship that herself did utter, but it sufficeth that your Lordship knoweth her Majesty's excellence and my weakness to express it; but I protest my heart was so filled with her kind speeches of your Lordship as I watered my eyes, and so craving always pardon, I rest every most dutifully.

Your Lordship's true poor friend to do you service.

C. HOWARD

The Court this Monday

Robert Devereux, Earl of Essex to Edward Dier**
July 21, 1587

On occasion Elizabeth enjoyed hurting and humiliating her servants, and she struck at Essex where she knew he was most sensitive—family pride. The Earl's sister, Dorothy, had eloped, and the Queeen, who believed in parental as well as royal authority, refused to receive her at court. In this letter Essex tells of how Elizabeth found herself in the same country house with Dorothy. He thus presents a rare picture of the Queen and of how difficult it could be to live with autocracy.

*From Henry Ellis, *Original Letters Illustrative of English History*, 3rd series (London, 1846), Vol. IV, pp. 148-149.
** From Walter B. Devereux, *Lives and Letters of the Devereux*, Vol. I, pp. 186-188.

MR. DIER, — I have been this morning at Winchester House to seek you, and I would have given a thousand pounds to have had one hour's speech with you; so much I would hearken to your counsel, and so greatly do I esteem your friendship. Things are fallen out very strangely against me, since my last being with you. Yesternight the Queen came to North Hall, where my Lady of Warwick would needs have my sister to be; which, though I knew not at the first, yet to prevent the worst, I made my Aunt Leighton signify so much unto the Queen..., that, at her coming to North Hall, this matter might not seem strange unto her. She seemed to be well pleased and well contented with it, and promised to use her well.

Yesternight, after she was come, and knew my sister was in the house, she commanded my Lady of Warwick that my sister should keep her chamber; whereupon, being greatly troubled in myself, I watched when the Queen had supped, to have some speech with her.... Her excuse was, first, she knew not of my sister's coming; and, besides, the jealousy that the world would conceive, that all her kindness to my sister was done for love of myself. Such bad excuses gave me a theme large enough, both for answer of them, and to tell her what the true causes were; why she would offer this disgrace both to me and to my sister, which was only to please that knave [Sir Walter] Ralegh, for whose sake I saw she would both grieve me and my love, and disgrace me in the eye of the world.

From thence she came to speak of Ralegh; and it seemed she could not well endure any thing to be spoken against him; and taking hold of one word, *disdain*, she said there was no such cause why I should disdain him. This speech did trouble me so much, that, as near as I could, I did describe unto her what he had been, and what he was; and then I did let her know whether I cause to disdain his competition of love, or whether I could have comfort to give myself over to the service of a mistress that was in awe of such a man. I spake, what of grief and choler, as much against him as I could, and I think he, standing at the door, might very well hear the worst that I spoke of himself. In the end, I saw she was resolved to defend him and to cross me. From thence she came to speak bitterly against my mother, which, because I could not endure to see me and my house disgraced (the only matter which both her choler and the practise of mine enemies had to work upon), I told her, for my sister she should not any longer disquiet her; I would, though it were almost midnight, send her away that night; and for myself, I had no joy to be in any place, but loath to be near about her, when I knew my affection so much thrown down, and such a wretch as Ralegh highly esteemed of her. To this she made not answer, but turned her away to my Lady of Warwick. So at that late hour I sent my men away with my sister; and after, I came hither myself. This strange alteration is by Ralegh's means; and the Queen, that hath tried all other ways, now will see whether she can by those hard courses drive me to be friends with Ralegh, which rather shall drive me to many other extremities.

If you come hither by twelve of the clock, I would fain speak with you. My resolution will let me take no longer time. I will be this night at Margate; and, if I can, I will ship myself for the Flushing. I will see Sluys lost or relieved, which cannot be yet, but is now ready to be done. If I return, I will be welcomed home; if not, *una bella morire,* is better than a disquiet life. This course may seem strange, but the extreme unkind dealing with me drives me to it. My friends will make the best of it; mine enemies cannot say it is unhonest; the danger is mine, and I am content to abide the worst. Whatsoever becomes of me, God grant her to be ever most happy; and so in haste I commit you to God.

Yours assured,
R. Essex.

Robert Devereux, Earl of Essex, to the Queen*
October 18, 1591

Essex was campaigning in France and wrote one of his many "love" letters to Elizabeth.

MOST FAIR, most dear, and most excellent Sovereign,.... At my departure I had a restless desire honestly to disengage myself from this French action; in my absence I conceive an assured hope to do something which shall make me worthy of the name of your servant; at my return I will humbly beseech your Maj. that no cause but a great action of your own may draw me out of your sight, for the two windows of your privy chamber shall be the poles of my sphere, where, as long as your Maj. will please to have me, I am fixed and unmovable. When your Maj. thinks that heaven too good for me, I will not fall like a star, but be consumed like a vapor by the same sun that drew me up to such a height. While your Maj. gives me leave to say I love you, my fortune is as my affection, unmatchable. If ever you deny me that liberty, you may end my life, but never shake my constancy, for were the sweetness of your nature turned into the greatest bitterness that could be, it is not in your power, as great a Queen as you are, to make me love you less. Therefore, for the honor of your sex, show yourself constant in kindness, for all your other virtues are confessed to be perfect; and so I beseech your Maj. receive all wishes of perfect happiness, from your Maj. most humble, faithful, and affectionate servant,

Dieppe, 18th Oct.

R. Essex.

Robert Devereux to the Lord Keeper Egerton**
October 18, 1598

Essex had had a serious quarrel with Elizabeth when she refused to listen to his advice. In a fury the Earl turned his back on his Queen; she told him to "be hanged" and boxed his ears; and Essex reached for his sword, realized the seriousness of the gesture and walked out of the room, swearing he would not have accepted such a face–slapping from Henry VIII himself. The Earl felt himself to be the aggrieved party despite the Lord Keeper's advice "to yield and submit to your sovereign, between whom and you there can be no proportion of duty."

*From Walter B. Devereux, *Lives and Letters of the Devereux*, Vol. I, pp. 249-250.
**Ibid.*, Vol. I, pp. 499-502.

MY VERY good Lord, — Although there is not that man this day living, whom I would sooner make a judge of any question that did concern me than yourself, yet must you give me leave to tell you, that in such a case I must appeal from all earthly judges; and if in any, then surely in this, where the highest judge on earth has imposed on me, without trial or hearing, the most heavy judgment that ever hath been known.... Your Lordship should rather condole with me than expostulate about the same.... There is no tempest comparable to the passionate indignation of a prince; nor yet at anytime is it so unseasonable, as when it lighteth upon those who might expect a harvest of their careful and painful labors. He that is once wounded must feel smart while his hurt be cured, or that the part be senseless; but no cure I expect, Her Majesty's heart being obdurate against me: and to be without sense I cannot, being made of flesh and blood...As for the two last objections, that I forsake my country when it hath most need of me, and fail in my indissoluble duty which I owe unto my sovereign, I answer, that if my country had at this time any need of my public service, Her Majesty, that governs the same, would not have driven me into a private kind of life. I am tied unto my country by two bands; in public place, to discharge faithfully, carefully, and industriously, the trust which is committed unto me; and the other private, to sacrifice for it my life and carcass which hath been nourished in it. Of the first I am freed, being dismissed, discharged, and disabled by Her Majesty. Of the other nothing can free me but death, and therefore no occasion of my performance shall offer itself, but I will meet it halfway. The indissoluble duty which I owe to Her Majesty is only the duty of allegiance, which I never will, nor never can, fail in. The duty of attendance is no indissoluble duty. I owe to Her Majesty the duty of an Earl and Lord Marshal of England. I have been content to do Her Majesty the service of a clerk, but can never serve her as a villain or slave. But yet, you say, I must give way unto the time. So I do; for now I see the storm come, I put myself into the harbor. Seneca saith, we must give place unto fortune; I know that fortune is both blind and strong, and therefore I go as far out of her way as I can. You say the remedy is, not to strive; I neither strive, nor seek for remedy. But, say you, I must yield and submit; I can neither yield myself to be guilty, or this imputation laid upon me to be just. I owe so much to the author of all truth, as I can never yield falsehood to be truth, nor truth falsehood.... I patiently bear all, and sensibly feel all, that I then received when this scandal was given me. Nay more, when the vilest of all indignities are done unto me, doth religion enforce me to sue? Doth God require it? Is it impiety not to do it? What, cannot princes err? Cannot subjects receive wrong? Is an earthly power or authority infinite? Pardon me, pardon we, my good Lord, I can never subscribe to these principles....As for me, I have received wrong, and feel it. My cause is good, I know it; and whatsoever come, all the powers on earth can never show more strength and constancy in oppressing, than I can show in suffering whatsoever can or shall be imposed on me.

Your Lordship in the beginning made yourself a looker on, and me a player of my own game; so you can see more than I can, yet must you give me leave to tell you in the end of my answer, that since you do but see, and I suffer, I must of necessity feel more than you do. I must crave your Lordship's patience to give him that hath a crabbed fortune, license to use a crabbed style; and yet whatsoever my style is there is no heart more humble to his superiors, nor any more affected to your Lordship, than that of your honor's poor friend,

Essex.

Robert Devereux, Earl of Essex to the Queen
May 12, 1600

Essex had badly bungled the Irish campaign and had returned to court against Elizabeth's explicit orders in order to explain his actions and failure. Not only was he placed under house arrest, but also the Queen refused to renew his monopoly on the import of sweet wines which, with an income of two to three thousand pounds a year, served as the financial basis for Essex' aristocratic existence. He could not survive without the Queen's bounty, and he and Elizabeth both knew it. In the next two letters the Earl had to force himself to grovel before the source of his economic well–being, for without the Queen's favor Essex was nothing despite his masculinity and ancient lineage.

BEFORE all letters written in this hand be banished, or he that sends this enjoin himself eternal silence, be pleased, I humbly beseech your Majesty, to read over these humble lines. At sundry times, and by sundry messengers, I received these words as your Majesty's own, that you meant to correct, and not to ruin; since which time, when I languished in four months sickness, forfeited almost all that I was able to engage, felt the very pangs of death upon me, and saw that poor reputation, whatsoever it was that I enjoyed hitherto, not suffered to die with me, but buried, and I alive, I yet kissed your Majesty's fair correcting hand, and was confident in your royal work; for I said to myself, between my ruin and my Sovereign's favor there is no mean, and if she bestow favor again, she gives it with all things that in this world I either need or desire. But now the length of my troubles, and the continuance, or rather increase, of your Majesty's indignation, have made all men so afraid of me, as mine own poor state is not only ruined, but my kind friends and faithful servants are like to die in prison, because I cannot help myself with mine own. Now, I do not only feel the weight of your Majesty's indignation, and am subject to their malicious insinuations that first envied me for my happiness in your favor, and now hate me out of custom; but as if I were thrown into a corner like a dead carcass, I am gnawed on and torn by the vilest and basest creatures upon earth. The prating tavern haunter speaks of me what he lists; the frantic libeller writes of me what he lists; already they print me and make me speak to the world, and shortly they will play me in what forms they list upon the stage. The least of these is a thousand times worse than death. But this is not the worst of my destiny, for your Majesty that hath mercy for all the world but me, that hath protected from scorn and infamy all to whom you ever avowed favor but Essex, and never repented you of any gracious assurance you had given till now; your Majesty, I say, hath now, in this eighth month of my close imprisonment, as if you thought mine infirmities, beggary, and infamy too little punishment, rejected my letters, and refused to hear of me, which to traitors you never did. What therefore remaineth for me? only this, to beseech your Majesty, on the knees of my heart, to conclude my punishment, my misery, and my life all

From Walter Devereux, *Lives and Letters of the Devereux,* Vol. II, pp. 98-99.

together, that I may go to my saviour, who hath paid himself a ransom for me, and whom, methinks, I still hear calling me out of this unkind world, in which I have lived too long, and ever thought myself too happy.

From your Majesty's humblest vassal,
12th May, 1600

Essex.

Robert Devereux, Earl of Essex to the Queen
November 17, 1600

VOUCHSAFE, dread Sovereign, to know there lives a man, though dead to the world, and in himself exercised with continued torments of mind and body, that doth more true honor to your thrice blessed day, than all those that appear in your sight. For no soul had ever such an impression of your perfections, no alteration showed such an effect of your power, nor no heart ever felt such a joy of your triumph. For they that feel that comfortable influence of your Majesty's favor, or stand in the bright beams of your presence, rejoice partly for your Majesty's, but chiefly for their own, happiness.

Only miserable Essex, full of pain, full of sickness, full of sorrow, languishing in repentance for his offences past, hateful to himself that he is yet alive, and importunate on death, if your sentence be irrevocable, he joys only for your Majesty's great happiness and happy greatness; and were the rest of his days never so many, and sure to be as happy as they are like to be miserable, he would lose them all to have this happy seventeenth day [i.e., the Queen's accession day] many and many times renewed with glory to your Majesty, and comfort of all your faithful subjects, of whom none is accursed but your Majesty's humblest vassal,

Essex

From Walter Devereux, *Lives and Letters of the Devereux*, Vol. II, p. 128.

IV. THE BENEFIT OF HINDSIGHT: THE HISTORIANS SPEAK

Sir Francis Bacon

THE CHARACTER OF QUEEN ELIZABETH

Francis Bacon (1561-1626) possessed one of the most original minds of the sixteenth century, and it is an interesting commentary on Elizabeth's personality that she never totally trusted him. Possibly Bacon lectured too much for the Queen's tastes; certainly he loved to give advice, and his voluminous writings are filled with counsel on everything from how to manipulate the sovereign and reform the legal system to the need for a new method of inquiry into the nature of things. Whatever the truth, Bacon was forever pestering and maneuvering for high office and was forever being turned down. Only after Elizabeth's death did he achieve his ambition, and eventually, in 1618, he was appointed Lord Chancellor by James I. [*formerly James VI of Scotland son of Mary Queen of Scots*] Under the circumstances the objectivity and perception of his evaluation of the Queen are remarkable. Written originally in Latin under the title of *In Felicem Memoriam Elizabethae Angliae Reginae,* it has been translated a number of times. The version given below in somewhat abbreviated form is from the 1696 edition of Bacon's *Essays*.

QUEEN ELIZABETH was one whom nature and fortune had made the wonder of her sex and an ornament to crowned heads....Every age has looked upon a female government as a rarity; if prosperous as a wonder; but if prosperous and long almost as a miracle. Whereas although she reigned full four and forty years, yet she outlived not her happiness. Of the happiness of her reign I design to say something, without running out into high encomiums. For praise indeed is the tribute of men, but happiness the gift of God.

I take this to be the first step to her happiness, that from a private condition she was raised to the administration of the regal power. Forasmuch as it is a standing rule in the morality and common sense of mankind that those things are to be looked upon as our greatest happiness which come beyond our hope and expectation. But this is not what I mean. That which I aim at is this, that princes, who are bred up in courts as the undoubted heirs of a crown, are so far debauched by a soft, indulgent and ef-feminate education, that they frequently become less capable of managing the state; whereas those have proved the best and most excellent princes, who have been under the discipline of both

Reprinted from Sir Francis Bacon, *The Essays...of Sir Francis Bacon, Lord Verulam, Viscount St. Albans* (London, 1696).

72   ELIZABETH I

fortunes. We need not go far for instances: Henry VII in England and Louis XII in France, within our own memory, and almost at the same time, mounted the throne, not only from a private but also from an adverse and harassed fortune; and the one proved famous for his prudence, the other for his justice. This was the case of Queen Elizabeth, whose fortune was as inconstant as the first, as at last when she came to the crown, it proved constant and even. For at her birth she was declared heiress to the throne, afterwards disinherited, and at last despised. During her brother's reign she enjoyed a more serene and favorable fortune, but whilst her sister swayed the scepter the clouds and storms returned upon her again. Nor was she advanced on a sudden from a prison to a throne, thereby to render her haughty after the provocation of her sufferings, but being restored to her liberty and raised in her hopes, she at last quietly and happily mounted the throne without any opposition or competitor....

Another part of the happiness of Queen Elizabeth seems to consist in the period and course of time wherein she reigned. Not only that it was long but because it was such a part of her life, as was most fit for managing the affairs of state, and governing a kingdom. For she was five and twenty years old when she began her reign...and she continued to reign to the 70th year of her age. So that she neither experienced what it was to be a minor, and under a governor's power; nor did she labor under the inconveniences of an extreme and miserable old age—an age, which even to private men brings too many troubles along with it; but to kings, beside the ordinary miseries of human life, it comes attended with the decay of their states, and is backed with an inglorious exist. For there has scarce been a king that has lived to an extreme and infirm old age but what lost much of that power and esteem, which he formerly had. Of this we have a notable instance in Philip II, King of Spain, a prince very

potent and one very skilled in the art of governing, who in his later days, laboring under the impotency of old age, deeply experienced the truth of what we asserted. He quitted all his conquests in France, made a peace with that nation, and endeavoured to do the same with others, that so he might leave all things in quiet and composed to his successors. On the other hand, Queen Elizabeth's fortune was so constant and vigorous that no declension of affairs followed her lively, though declining, age. Nay more, for a standing and most certain monument of her happiness, she died not before a victory in Ireland had put an end to the rebellion there, so shining and so uniform was her glory in all its parts! Besides, I think it very material to reflect over what sort of people she bore the sway, for had her government been over the Palmyrenians, or any other soft and unmanly nation of Asia, it had been a less wonder, since a female in the throne would be suitable enough to an effeminate people, but to have all things move and be directed by a woman's nod in England, a nation so fierce and warlike; this, I say, justly raises our highest admiration.

But although the genius of her subjects was so desirous of war, and so impatient of peace, yet this did not hinder her from maintaining it strictly all her reign. And this natural inclination of hers, joined with success, is what I reckon redounds to her highest commendation. For this conduced much to the happiness of her own life, to the honor of her sex, and to the peace and quiet of her conscience. About the tenth year of her reign, an insurrection was indeed attempted in the north, but it was soon hushed and suppressed. All the rest of her time England enjoyed a secure and profound peace. And I account it a most glorious peace, upon these two accounts....The first is, that it appeared the more conspicuous and shining by the calamities of its neighbors, which were all in flames round about it. Another is, that even in the

Everywhere around there was turmoil, except in England.

blessings of peace there still remained so much martial glory, as by its famous actions not only retained but likewise increased the honor of the English nation. For the supplies sent into the Netherlands, France and Scotland; the voyages that were made to the Indies and round the whole world; the fleets that were sent to infest Portugal and the coasts of Spain, and the Irish rebels so often conquered and cut off, were all sufficient testimonies that England had remitted and lost nothing of its ancient glory in the field of war....

There is still another reason why we should admire the peaceful reign of Queen Elizabeth, namely because the peace which she enjoyed was not owing to the inclination which the age she lived in had to it, but wholly to her own prudence and wise conduct. She struggled with an inbred faction at home, upon the account of religion; and the strength of the kingdom, like the common bulwark of all Europe, seemed to oppose the growing greatness of the Spaniard, and his ambition so formidable at that time; so that upon these accounts, there was a sufficient cause of war, but by her forces and policy she surmounted these difficulties. This was demonstrated by one of the most memorable events that ever happened in the whole course of affairs of our age. For when the Spanish Armada rode upon our seas, to the terror of all Europe, with so much noise and so much assurance of success, it took not the least Fisher-boat nor burnt the least cottage, nor so much as touched upon our coast; but being routed in an engagement, was dispersed by a miserable flight, and with frequent storms; and so left England and her seacoast in an unmoved and undisturbed peace. Nor was she less fortunate in disappointing the secret plots of her private foes, than in conquering and routing the forces of an open enemy. For although there were many conspiracies laid against her life, yet were they most happily discovered and defeated. Nor was she upon that account more fearful or anxious of the safety of her person; her guards were not increased, nor did she confine herself in her palace without appearing abroad. But secure of herself and trusting to her subjects, she remembered her deliverance, but forgot the danger, and altered nothing of her usual management and behavior.

It is likewise worth our observation to consider in what sort of times she flourished. For some ages are so barbarous and ignorant that men have been governed with as much ease as a shepherd drives and manages his sheep. But this princess lived in a most learned and polite age; wherein it required great parts and a high degree of virtue to be excellent. A female government is likewise very often eclipsed by marriage, and all the praises and conduct is bestowed upon the husband; whilst those who live unmarried have no sharers or partners in their glory. And in this was our Queen the more to be commended in that her throne stood upon no other basis than what she herself had erected. She had no brother, no uncle, nor any other of the royal family, to partake of her cares or share in her government. But even those whom she did advance to any places of trust were so managed and kept in such awe that each of them was solicitous how to please her; so that she was always mistress of herself. She was indeed childless, and left no issue of her own body to succeed her, but this has been the case of the most fortunate princes, of Alexander the Great, of Julius Caesar, of Trajan, and several others; which has been variously censured and has always been a matter of dispute. For some have looked upon it as a diminution of human happiness, as if men should not be completely happy unless they were so both in their own persons and in the propagation of their species; but others have esteemed it as the greater happiness because then it seems to be complete, when it is not any longer subjected to the various turns of fortune, which it is impossible to secure when a posterity is left behind.

To all this we may add her outward embellishments; she was tall of stature, well shaped in her body, and had in her face the mixture of sweetness and majesty; and always enjoyed a very sound health. Besides all this, she was strong and vigorous to the very last, never experienced the changes of fortune nor the miseries of old age, and at last by an easy and gentle death she obtained that euthanasia, which Augustus Caesar used to desire so passionately. This also is recorded of Antoninus Pius, one of the best emperors, whose death seemed to be nothing else but a quiet and sweet slumber. Just so in Queen Elizabeth's distemper, there was nothing that was deadly, or ominous, or unsuitable to humane nature. She was not desirous of life, or impatient under sickness, nor disturbed with the tortures of any pain. No direful, no pestilential symptom appeared, but everything seemed rather to prognosticate the decay of nature, than either the corruption or disparagement of it. For some few days before her death, being weakened by the dryness of her constitution, and the cares of the government, having not so much as drank any wine or taken any moist diet, she was seized with dead palsy, but yet (which is not usual in that distemper) she retained her speech, her sense and her motion, although not so brisk and lively as before. Nor was she long in this condition, so that it did not seem to be the last act of her life, but rather the first step to her death. For although it is esteemed a misery to live a long time in the loss of the use of our faculties; yet to be prepared for death by a gradual decay of our senses is certainly a very sweet and pleasant dissolution.

Another remarkable addition to her happiness is this, that she was not only very happy in her own person but likewise in the worthiness of her ministers of state. For she made choice of such men as this Island perhaps was never so happy in before. But God that favors kings, raises them up ministers and adorns their minds.

There remain two posthumous felicities, which seem to attend the more noble and august passages of her life: the one is that of her successor, the other that of her memory. For she has got such a successor who, though by his masculine virtue and offspring and late accession to the throne, he may eclipse her glory; yet is so far a favorer of her name and esteem, and is so willing to transmit her actions to posterity, that he has made little alterations, either in the choice of ministers or in the method of governing. So that hardly any father has been succeeded by his son with less noise, disturbance or alteration. As for her memory, it is so much in the mouths and so fresh in the minds of all men, that death seems to have extinguished envy and put her fame in a clearer light, and now the happiness of her memory does as it were strive to outvie that of her life....Nor could that happiness we have been describing be attained by any but such as are supported and highly indulged by the divine favor, and such in some measure by their morals and virtue are the establishers of their own fortune. However I thought fit to subjoin some few hints and respects to those morals of the Queen, which seem to have been most exposed to the lash of malevolent tongues.

In religion, Queen Elizabeth was pious and moderate, constant and steady, and a profest enemy to novelty. As for her piety, though the chief strokes of it appeared in the actions and affairs of state, yet some signs of it were to be seen in the course of her life, and her ordinary conversation. She was seldom absent from divine service, either in her public or private chapel. She employed much of her time in reading the Scriptures and the writings of the Fathers, especially of St. Augustine. She composed some prayers herself, upon some occasions and for some extraordinary purpose. Whenever she mentioned the name of

God, even in ordinary discourse, she generally added the title of creator; and showed some sort of humility and reverence in her looks and countenance, which I myself have often observed. As for that which some have reported, that she was so far from thinking of her mortality that she could not endure to be told of old age or death, it is absolutely false; since she herself, several years before her death, would frequently with much facetiousness call herself the old woman, and would often discourse about the inscription she had a mind should be upon her tomb. She gave out that she was no lover of glory and pompous titles, but only desired her memory might be recorded in a line or two, which should very briefly express her name, her virginity, the time of her reign, the reformation of religion, and her preservation of the peace. Tis true, in the flower of her age before she was past childbearing, when she was importuned by some to declare her successor, she did make answer that she could by no means endure to have a shroud held before her eyes while she was living....

As for her moderation in religion, perhaps in this her character will deem deficient, because of the severity of those laws which were made against her subjects of the Romish religion; but we will produce such things, as are well known to us, and carefully taken notice of by us. This is certain, that she was always averse from laying any constraint on men's consciences, but yet she could not allow that the government should be endangered under the pretense of conscience and religion. Hence it was that she thought nothing but a certain destruction would ensue if she should at the first grant a liberty and toleration of two religions by public authority to a fierce and headstrong people, who would soon upon their private animosities fall together by the ears. Even in the beginning of her reign, when all things looked with a suspicious face, she kept some of the prelates, which were of a more turbulent and factious spirit, prisoners at large, though she had the law on her side; and to the rest of both orders, she used not any sharp inquisition but by a generous connivance kept them under her protection. This was the posture of affairs at first. Nor did she swerve much from this clemency, though provoked by the Bull of Excommunication, thundered against her by Pius V. This indeed might have raised her indignation, and have been the occasion of new modeling the state, but still she retained her own generous temper. For this prudent and courageous woman was not much moved at the noise of such threatenings, being secure of the fidelity and affection of her subjects, and not fearing any harm from the Romish faction, which was too weak to attempt anything unless seconded by a foreign enemy.

But about the three and twentieth year of her reign, the face of affairs was quite changed. Nor is this period of time, feigned to serve a turn only but mentioned in public records and engraven as it were in leaves of brass. Nor were her subjects of the Romish religion punished with any severity before that year, though several laws had formerly been enacted against them. But at this time it was by degrees discovered what vast and ambitious designs were laid by Spain to conquer this kingdom. A great part of this design was to raise a faction in the very heart of the nation, which being no friends to the government, and desirous of alteration, should join with the enemy upon his invasion. This was hoped would be effected upon the difference there was in religion; whereupon they resolved to improve that breach, and priests were sent over from the young seminaries to raise and increase men's love for the Romish religion, to teach and enforce the validity of the Pope's bull, which absolved the Queen's subjects from their allegiance, and to excite and prepare the minds of men for an alteration in the government....

In a time of so much danger, Queen

Elizabeth was obliged by a kind of fatal necessity to enact severe laws, thereby to restrain those of her subjects, who being averse to her government and grown past the hopes of being cured, began to grow rich by the private life they led, being exempted from the charge and burden of public offices. The origin of this spreading evil was charged upon the seminary priests, who were bred up in foreign parts and maintained by the charity and benevolence of foreign princes, the profest enemies of the realm; who had lived in places where the best titles they could bestow on Queen Elizabeth were those of heretic, excommunicated and damnable fury; who though they themselves were not engaged in treasonable practices, yet were known to be the intimate friends of such as were guilty of those villainies; and who, by their artifices and poisonous methods had depraved the very sacrifice of the mass, which before was a sweet and harmless thing, and had as it were infected it with a new kind of ferment and pernicious malignity. Whereupon the only expedient to put a stop to this growing evil was thought to be the prohibiting these men from coming into the land upon pain of death; which was accordingly enacted in the seven and twentieth year of her reign. Nor did the event itself, when so great a storm broke out upon and threatened the nation, in the least take off from the envy and hatred of these men, but rather increased it; so far had they divested themselves of the love they owed their country. Afterwards when our fears of Spain (the true occasion of this severity) were over and vanished, yet the memory of the former times was so deeply fixed in the minds and senses of most men, and to have abrogated the laws that were once made would have argued so much inconstancy, or to have slighted them would have been a sign of so much indifference; that Queen Elizabeth as cases then stood did not think it safe for herself that things should return to the same posture they were in before the three and twentieth year of her reign....However, she (to glory of her good nature be it spoken) did so far blunt the edge of the laws that but very few priests suffered death upon that account....But not to forget what we first asserted; we think we have abundantly demonstrated that she was moderate in points of religion, and that the alteration which did happen was not owing to her nature but to the iniquity of the times.

Of her constancy in religion and worship thereof, the greatest proof is that with an undaunted mind and little assistance she extirpated and abrogated the Romish religion, as being disagreeable to the word of God, the primitive purity and her own conscience; notwithstanding in her sister's reign it was established by public authority and a great deal of care, and had taken deep root, and was strengthened with the consent and approbation of all that were in authority and places of trust. Nor did she do this hastily or in a heat, but cautiously and by degrees. The truth of which appears not only in her whole conduct of affairs but also in that answer which she once made to a courtier upon the like occasion. For in the beginning of her reign, when according to the custom the prisoners were to be released to grace and honor her first accession to the throne, as she was going to chapel she was accosted by a certain courtier, who took more than ordinary freedom, being of a pleasant and facetious nature. He, either prompted to it by his own private inclination, or set on by a wiser head, delivered a petition into her hand, and in a full concourse of people with a loud voice expressed himself thus. That there were still four or five kept prisoners, and that for no reason at all. That he came to petition for their freedom as well as for the rest. That they were the four Evangelists, and Apostle St. Paul, who had been long confined in an unknown tongue, as it were in a prison, and were not suffered to appear abroad in the world. The Queen gave him this very cautious reply: That it was best to consult them first, whether they were willing to have their freedom yet, or no. And thus she kept everything within her own power, by giving such a doubtful answer to so surprising a demand. Nor did she carry on things fearfully, and by fits and starts, but gravely, orderly and maturely. A conference first had between the parties, and a parliament first called, and at last, within the compass of a year, she so far ordered and established all things which concerned religion, that she did not suffer the least title of them to be altered, during all her reign. And it was always her public admonition in almost every session of Parliament that no innovation should be made in the discipline and ceremonies of the church. Thus far of her religion.

Now if any of the graver sort should object these levities: "that she was contented and desirous to be admired, to be courted and upon the account of love to be praised and extolled; and that she continued these levities even to an age wherein they were unbecoming her." Yet if you take even these in a milder sense, they are not without their due admiration, since they are such things as often are to be found in the fabulous narrations of poets and others. Thus it is recorded of a certain queen in the fortunate islands, who in her court and government entertained that soft thing called love, and yet forbade lust to enter there. But if a harsher construction should be put upon them, yet they are to be admired, and that very highly too, since these softnesses cast but little blemish on her fame, and none at all upon her grandeur, did no injury to her government, and hindered not the public administration of affairs. For these sorts of things are usually joined to the most noted fortune. But to conclude this essay; she was certainly a good, moral princess, and as such she desired to appear. She was a hater of vice, and studied to grow famous by honorable methods. And truly at the naming of her manners, something comes into my mind, which I will here declare. When she had ordered an express to be written to her Ambassador, concerning certain instructions which he was privately to impart to the Queen Mother of France at Valois, and her Secretary had inserted a certain clause that the Ambassador to ingratiate himself the better should say—That they were two female princes, of whom in the management of affairs and in the art and skill of governing, as great things were expected as from the best of men—she struck out and said that she used quite different arts and methods in the administration of the government. And she was extremely pleased when anyone by chance dropped out such an expression as this—That she would have lived and excelled in the eye of the world, though she had spent her days in a private and mean station. So desirous was she that nothing of her virtue and praise should be owing to the grandeur of her fortune. But if I should enter upon praises, either moral or political, or should touch only upon her virtues, which would be a disparagement to so great a princess; or should I endeavour to set them in their clear and proper light, I must run out into the history of her life, which requires more leisure, and a larger genius than I can pretend to. For I have here given you her character in short. But it must after all be said, that only time will bestow a true encomium on this excellent woman, since no age since the creation could ever show her equal in her own sex, that was so fit to manage the affairs of a state.

James Anthony Froude

THE REIGN OF ELIZABETH

For almost half a century, James Anthony Froude (1818-1894) dominated Tudor historiography both because of the magnitude of his scholarly output (twelve volumes on the sixty years between 1528 and 1588) and because he was the target of bitter criticism directed at his views on Henry VIII, Elizabeth, and the Reformation, his approach to history, and the quality of his scholarship. His *History of England from the Fall of Wolsey to the Defeat of the Spanish Armada* was published between 1856 and 1870, and by the time he had concluded his opus Froude had decided what history was all about. It was high drama in which the role of the historian was simply to "let his story tell itself in the deeds and words of those who acted it out." He was fascinated by the reactions of contemporaries to the events surrounding them, and he produced a narrative which still makes magnificent reading. Starting with a strong bias in favor of the English Reformation, he sought to show that not only was the Reformation a good thing in itself, but also that it was handled with skill and judgment by men and women whose descendants would later on prove again the vigor and genius of the Anglo-Saxon as he spread British institutions, values, and virtues throughout the world. Henry VIII is clearly the hero of the story, while Elizabeth, somewhat to Froude's embarrassment, emerges as an intriguing but essentially second-rate female who was difficult to live with, parsimonious to a dangerous extreme, and fatally susceptible to flattery and a well-turned calf. The more Froude read and translated the documents—and he did so with a vigor and thoroughness not equalled until the twentieth century—the more he became "a Cecil maniac," believing that it was William Cecil, not the Queen, who received the credit. Yet Froude was honest enough to admit that Elizabeth, for all her failings, had the sense to follow Cecil's advice and not that of worthless flatterers and court favorites.

HER CHARACTER I have left to be gathered from her actions, from her letters, from the communications between herself and her ministers, and from the opinions expressed freely to one another in private by those ministers themselves. The many persons with whom she was brought into confidential relations during her long reign, noted down what she said to them, and her words have been brought up in judgment against her; and there have been extremely few men and women in this world whose lives would bear so close a scrutiny, or who could look forward to being subjected to it without shame and

From James Anthony Froude, *History of England from the Fall of Wolsey to the Defeat of the Spanish Armada* (New York, 1878), Vol. XII, pp. 580-587.

dismay. The mean thoughts which cross the minds and at one time or other escape from the lips of most of us, were observed and remembered when proceeding from the mouth of a sovereign, and rise like accusing spirits in authentic frightfulness out of the private drawers of statesmen's cabinets. Common persons are sheltered by obscurity; the largest portion of their faults they forget themselves, and others do not care to recollect: while kings and queens are at once refused the ordinary allowances for human weakness, and pay for their great place in life by a trial before posterity more severe it is to be hoped than awaits us all at the final Judgment-bar.

This, too, ought to be borne in mind: that sovereigns, when circumstances become embarrassing, may not, like unvalued persons, stand aside and leave others to deal with them. Subjects are allowed to decline responsibility, to refuse to undertake work which they dislike, or to lay down at any time a burden which they find too heavy for them. Princes born to govern find their duties cling to them as their shadows. Abdication is often practically impossible. Every day they must do some act or form some decision from which consequences follow of infinite moment. They would galdly do nothing if they might, but it is not permitted to them. They are denied the alternative of inaction, which is so often the best safeguard against doing wrong.

Elizabeth's situation was from the very first extremely trying. She had few relation, none of any weight in the State, and those whom like Hunsdon and Sir Francis Knollys she took into her Cabinet, derived their greatness from herself. Her unlucky, it may be almost called culpable, attachment to Leicester made marriage unconquerably distasteful to her, and her disappointment gave an additional twist to her natural eccentricities. Circumstances more than choice threw her originally on the side of the Reformation, and when she told the Spanish Ambassadors that she had been forced into the separation from the Papacy against her will, she probably spoke but the truth. She was identified in her birth with the cause of independence. The first battle had been fought over her cradle, and her right to be on the throne turned mortally, if not in law, on the legitimacy of Queen Catherine's divorce. Her sister had persecuted her as the child of the woman who had caused her mother so much misery, and her friends, therefore, had naturally been those who were most her sister's enemies. She could not have submitted to the Pope without condemning her father, or admitting a taint upon her own birth, while in Mary of Scotland she had a rival ready to take advantage of any concession which she might be tempted to make.

For these reasons, and not from any sympathy with the views either of Luther or Calvin, she chose her party at her accession. She found herself compelled against her will to become the patron of heretics and rebels, in whose objects she had no interest, and in whose theology she had no belief. She resented the necessity while she submitted to it, and her vacillations are explained by the reluctance with which each successive step was forced upon her, on a road which she detested. It would have been easy for a Protestant to be decided. It would have been easy for a Catholic to be decided. To Elizabeth the speculations of so-called divines were but as ropes of sand and sea-slime leading to the moon, and the doctrines for which they were rending each other to pieces a dream of fools or enthusiasts. Unfortunately her keenness of insight was not combined with any profound concern for serious things. She saw through the emptiness of the forms in which religion presented itself to the world. She had none the more any larger or deeper conviction of her own. She was without the intellectual emotions which give human character its consistency and power. One moral quality she possessed in an eminent degree: she was supremely brave. For thirty years she was perpetually a mark for assassination, and her spirits were never affected, and she was never frightened into cruelty. She had a proper contempt also for idle luxury and indulgence. She lived simply, worked hard, and ruled her household with rigid economy. But her vanity was as insatiable as it was commonplace. No flattery was too tawdry to find a welcome with her, and as she had no repugnance to false words in others, she was equally liberal of them herself. Her entire nature was saturated with artifice. Except when speaking some round untruth Elizabeth never could be simple. Her letters and her speeches were as fantastic as her dress, and her meaning as involved as her policy. She was unnatural even in her prayers, and she carried her affectations into the presence of the Almighty. She might doubt legitimately whether she ought to assist an Earl of Murray or a Prince of Orange when in arms against their sovereign; but her scruples extended only to the fulfillment of her promises of support, when she had herself tempted them into insurrection. Obligations of honour were not only occasionally forgotten by her, but she did not seem to understand what honour meant.

Vain as she was of her own sagacity, she never modified a course recommended to her by Burghley without injury both to the realm and to herself. She never chose an opposite course without plunging into embarrassments, from which his skill and Walsingham's were barely able to extricate her. The great results of her reign were the fruits of a policy which was not her own, and which she starved and mutilated when energy and completeness were needed.

That she pushed no question to extremities, that, for instance, she refused to allow the succession to the crown to be determined, and permitted the Catholics to expect the accession of the Queen of Scots has been interpreted by the result into wisdom. She gained time by it, and her hardest problems were those which

time alone could resolve satisfactorily. But the fortune which stood her friend so often never served her better than in lengthening her life into old age. Had the Queen of Scots survived her, her legacy to England would have been a desperate and dreadful civil war, and her reluctance was no result of any farsighted or generous calculation. She wished only to reign in quiet till her death, and was contented to leave the next generation to settle its own difficulties. Her tenderness towards conspirators was as remarkable as it was hitherto unexampled; but her unwillingness to shed blood extended only to high–born traitors. Unlike her father, who ever struck the leaders and spared the followers, Elizabeth could rarely bring herself to sign the death-warrant of a nobleman; yet without compunction she could order Yorkshire peasants to be hung in scores by martial law. Mercy was the quality with which she was most eager to be credited. She delighted in popularity with the multitude, and studied the conditions of it; but she uttered no word of blame, she rather thanked the perpetrators for good service done to the commonwealth, when Essex sent in his report of the women and children who were stabbed in the caves of Rathlin. She was remorseless when she ought to have been most forbearing, and lenient when she ought to have been stern; and she owed her safety and her success to the incapacity and the divisions of her enemies, rather than to wisdom and resolution of her own. Time was her friend, time and the weakness of Philip; and the fairest feature in her history, the one relation in which from first to last she showed sustained and generous feeling, is that which the perversity of history has selected as the blot on her escutcheon. Beyond and beside the political causes which influenced Elizabeth's attitude towards the Queen of Scots, true human pity, true kindness, a true desire to save her from herself, had a real place. From the day of Mary Stuart's marriage with Francis II the English throne was the dream of her imagination, and the means to arrive at it her unceasing practical study. Any contemporary European sovereign, any English sovereign in an earlier age, would have deemed no means unjustifiable to remove so perilous a rival. How it would have fared with her after she came to England, the fate of Edward II, of Richard, of Henry VI, of the Princes in the Tower, and later yet, of the unhappy son of the unhappy Clarence might tell. Whatever might have been the indirect advantage of Mary Stuart's prospective title, the danger from her presence in the realm must have infinitely exceeded it. She was "the bosom serpent," "the thorn in the flesh," which could not be plucked out; and after the Rebellion of the North, and the discovery of the Ridolfi conspiracy, neither Philip nor Alva expected that she would be permitted to survive. It seems as if Elizabeth, remembering her own danger in her sister's lifetime, had studied to show an elaborate tenderness to a person who was in the same relation to herself. From the beginning to the end no trace can be found of personal animosity on the part of Elizabeth; on the part of Mary no trace of anything save the fiercest hatred.

But this, like all other questions connected with the Virgin Queen, should be rather studied in her actions than in the opinion of the historian who relates them. Actions and words are carved upon eternity. Opinions are but forms of cloud created by the prevailing currents of the moral air. Princes, who are credited on the wrong side with the evils which happen in their reigns, have a right in equity to the honour of the good. The greatest achievement in English history, the "breaking the bonds of Rome," and the establishment of spiritual independence, was completed without bloodshed under Elizabeth's auspices, and Elizabeth may have the glory of the work. Many problems growing out of it were left unsettled. Some were disposed of on the scaffold at Whitehall, some in the revolution of 1688; some yet survive to test the courage and the ingenuity of modern politicians.

But the worst legacy which princes or statesmen could bequeath to their country would be the resolution of all its perplexities, the establishment once and for ever of a finished system, which would neither require nor tolerate improvement.

Mandell Creighton

THE LAST YEARS OF ELIZABETH

Mandell Creighton (1843-1901), the son of a master carpenter, by sheer intelligence succeeded in becoming one of Britain's most distinguished historians and churchmen. Born in 1843, he was appointed to the chair of ecclesiastical history at Cambridge in 1884,

From Mandell Creighton, *Queen Elizabeth* (London, 1899), pp. 197-200.

and was a founder and first editor of the *English Historical Review*. In 1890 he was created Bishop of Peterborough; seven years later he was named Bishop of London. Creighton's greatest—certainly his longest—work was his six–volume *History of the Papacy*; but his short, entertaining, and astute biography of Queen Elizabeth, originally published in 1896, remains his masterpiece. Creighton admired but was never captivated by Gloriana, and though he imposed upon her and her times his own deeply felt patriotism and confidence in Britain's achievements, his evaluation of the Queen is by far the least anachronistic and moralistic account by any of the nineteenth-century English historians.

THE CHARACTER of Elizabeth is difficult to detach from her actions. She represented England as no other ruler ever did. For the greater part of her long reign the fortunes of England absolutely depended upon her life, and not only the fortunes of England, but those of Europe as well. If England had passed under the Papal sway it is hard to see how Protestantism could have survived the repressive forces to which it would have been exposed. There were times when Elizabeth doubted if this could be avoided, times when any one, save Anne Boleyn's daughter, would have been tempted to make terms. In asking England to rally round her Elizabeth knew that she could not demand any great sacrifices on her behalf. By cultivating personal loyalty, by demanding it in exaggerated forms, she was not merely feeding her personal vanity; she was creating a habit which was necessary for the maintenance of her government. By avoiding risky undertakings, by keeping down public expense, she was not merely indulging her tendency to parsimony; she was warding off from her people demands which they were unequal at that time to sustain.

Elizabeth's imperishable claim to greatness lies in her instinctive sympathy with her people. She felt, rather than understood, the possibilities which lay before England, and she set herself the task of slowly exhibiting, and impressing them on the national mind. She educated Englishmen to a perception of England's destiny, and for this purpose fixed England's attention upon itself. She caught at every advantage which was afforded by the divided condition of Europe to assert England's importance. France and Spain alike had deep causes of hostility; she played off one against the other, so that both were anxious for the friendship of a State which they each hoped some day to annex. England gained courage from this sight and grew in self-confidence. To obtain this result Elizabeth was careless of personal dignity or honour. She did not care how her conduct was judged at the time, but awaited the result.

It is this faculty of intuitive sympathy with her people which makes Elizabeth so difficult to understand in details of her policy. The fact was that she never faced a question in the shape in which it presented itself. It was true that it had to be recognised and discussed in that form; but Elizabeth had no belief in a policy because it could be clearly stated and promised well. Things had to be discussed, and decisions arrived at in consequence of such discussion; but action could always be avoided at the last moment, and Elizabeth would never act unless she felt that her people were in hearty agreement with her. Thus in her position towards her ministers she represented in her own person the vacillations and fluctuations of popular opinion. Ministers naturally wish to have an intelligible policy. Burghley laboriously drew up

* stinginess

papers which balanced the advantages and disadvantages of alternative courses of action. Elizabeth read them and seemed to accept one out of two inevitable plans. She felt that, as a reasonable being, she could not do otherwise. But when it came to decisive action she fell back upon her instinctive perception of what England wanted. As she could not explain this, she was driven to all sorts of devices to gain time. She could not, on the other hand, fully take her people into her confidence. It was the unconscious tendency of their capacities which she interpreted, not their actual demands. She was eliciting from them their meaning, and educating them to understand it themselves. For this purpose she must seem to govern more absolutely than she did; but on great occasions, she took them into her confidence, and fired them with a high conception of the greatness of their national life. She strove to focus and coordinate all their aspirations, and only repressed tendencies which were adverse to the formation of an English spirit; for she cared more for the spirit of the national life than for its outward organization.

Her private character is hard to detach from her public character. She behaved to those around her as she did to her people in general. She was surrounded by men representative of English life; they must be made to fall into line; and any method which served this purpose was good. Above all things she must impose her will equally on all. Personally, she was attracted by physical endowments, and let herself go in accordance with her feelings up to a certain point. But she was both intellectually and emotionally cold. In politics and in private life alike she cared little for decorum,* because she knew that she could stop short whenever prudence made it needful.

It is easy to point out serious faults in Elizabeth, to draw out her inconsistencies, and define her character in a series of paradoxes. But this treatment does not exhibit the real woman, still less the real Queen. Elizabeth was hailed at her accession as being "mere English"; and "mere English" she remained. Round her, with all her faults, the England which we know grew into the consciousness of its destiny. The process was difficult; the struggle was painful, and it left many scars behind. There are many things in Elizabeth which we could have wished otherwise; but she saw what England might become, and nursed it into the knowledge of its power.

*polite behavior

Joseph Hilaire Pierre René Belloc

QUEEN ELIZABETH

Hilaire Belloc (1870-1953) was born to a French father and an English, Unitarian mother (who converted to Catholicism), and he later married an American. Radical in politics, outspoken on a host

From Hilaire Belloc, *Characters of the Reformation* (London: Sheed and Ward, 1936), pp. 108-115. Reprinted by permission of the publisher.

of controversial subjects, and blessed with a stamina which permitted him to turn out ten to twelve thousand words in a single morning's work, Belloc wrote well over a hundred novels, histories, biographies and collections of poems, short stories and essays. He was a vigorous defender of Catholicism, seeing Europe—its history and civilization—as the unique creation of the Roman Catholic Church. He has no standing in the eyes of professional historians, for Belloc scorned footnotes and tended to confuse verifiable facts with personal opinions. As one historian has commented, Belloc's interpretation of Elizabeth and the sixteenth century has "if...nothing else, the quality of novelty." Obviously, Belloc must be read with caution. Nevertheless, his sketch of the Queen is included in this book of readings for several reasons: first, it is evidence that religion even in the twentieth century is a crucial factor in conditioning our view of the past; and second, Belloc was one of the few writers to concern himself with a cardinal phenomenon about Elizabeth's life—the myth which it has engendered. The selection presented here is from a delightful, sometimes scurrilous, and always biased little book entitled *Characters of the Reformation*, published in 1936. Needless to say, Elizabeth was not one of Belloc's favorite characters.

THE INTEREST of Queen Elizabeth to the historian is mainly biographical; but it has also the interest of a myth.

The interest is mainly biographical because she was of very little effect upon the history of her time. We do not find any great political events produced by her will or her intelligence and there is nothing important in the Europe of her time or the England of her time of which we can say, "This was done by Elizabeth."

But the woman herself is so interesting, not only as a pathological case but as an example of suffering and intelligence combined, of a warped temperament and all that goes with it, that, biographically, she is a first-rate subject and one which, it may be added, has never been properly dealt with. There is no one well-known book which gives an even approximately true picture of Elizabeth; at least, none in the English language.

The reason of this is due to the presence of that other interest in her character, the myth. What may be called "The Elizabethan Myth" is only now beginning to break down, and it was during the nineteenth century an article of faith in England (and, through England, elsewhere). It is one of the most perfect modern examples of its kind in all the range of history. It is a sort of creative and vital falsehood, radiating its effects upon all the details of the time, and putting in the wrong light pretty well everything that happened.

The Elizabethan myth may be stated thus:

"In the second half of the sixteenth century England had the good fortune to be governed by a woman of strong will, powerful intelligence and excellent judgment, whose power was supreme. Her people adored her, and produced in her time and largely under her influence the greatest figures in every sphere: literature, architecture, foreign politics and the rest. She chose her ministers with admirable skill and they served her with corresponding faithfulness. In consequence of all this the Great Queen led the nation through paths of increasing prosperity; it grew wealthier and wealthier as her reign proceeded, more and more powerful abroad, founding colonies and establishing that command of the sea which England has never since lost. In religion she wisely represented the strong Protestantism of her people in hatred of which a few venomous rebels—shamefully allied with foreigners—attacked her reign and even her life. However, she easily triumphed over them all and died full of glory, leaving her name as that of the greatest of the English sovereigns.''

There in brief is the "Elizabethan Myth," and a more monstrous scaffolding of poisonous nonsense has never been foisted on posterity. I use the word "poisonous" not at random, not as a mere epithet of abuse, but with a full sense of its accuracy; for this huge falsehood which might be merely absurd in another connection has had, applied to English history, all the effect that a poison has upon a living body. It has interfered with the proper scale of history, it has twisted, altered and denied the most obvious historical truths and has given Englishmen and even the world at large a false view of our past.

The myth is now beginning to break down. It could not survive detailed and critical work. Moreover, I perceive a danger that in its breakdown there will be too strong a reaction the other way and that men when they find out how they have been duped will run to the opposite extreme, and perhaps come to believe that Elizabeth was insignificant.

Whatever she was she was not that. Her position was weak, but she herself was not weak.

The truth about Elizabeth is this. She was the puppet or figurehead of the group of new millionaires established upon the loot of religion begun in her father's time. They had at their head the unique genius of William Cecil, who, in spite of dangerous opposition, accomplished what might have seemed the impossible task of digging up the Catholic faith by the roots from English soil, stamping out the Mass, and shepherding the younger generation of a reluctant people into a new religious mood.

Throughout her life Elizabeth was thwarted in each political effort she made; she felt the check of her masters and especially Cecil as a horse feels the bridle. She never had her will in matters of state.

In personal history the truth about Elizabeth is that she was a woman of strong will and warped by desperately bad bodily health, almost certainly by a secret abnormality which forbade her to bear children. This wretched health, to which half a dozen times in her life she nearly succumbed, partly accounted for a mind also diseased on the erotic side. It is not a pleasant subject, and not one on which I can dwell at length in these pages, but it must be very strongly emphasized for it accounts for all her intimate life and all that was most characteristic of her from her fifteenth year.

Her relations with men were continual, but they were not normal and they were the more scandalous for that. Like others who have suffered the same tragic disease of perversion in mind and body it seemed to increase upon her with age. Already within sight of the grave and approaching her seventieth year she was shamefully associated with one whom she had taken up as a lad, a young fellow nearly thirty-three years her junior. Her intellect was high and piercing, she had real wit, very full instruction in many languages, and her will, in spite of perpetual rebuffs, remained strong to the end, though woefully impotent to carry into effect.

No one chafed more or suffered more under the domination of others than Elizabeth, and no one has had to accept it more thoroughly. She had, on this side of the intelligence and of the will, only one weakness, but that so exaggerated that it was hardly sane. She insisted upon flattery, and particularly upon flattery which was so exaggerated as to be absurd. She certainly was not taken in by it, but she seems to have had a maniac appetite for it, liking it the more the more she knew it to be absurd. When she had long been dried up and wizened, with skin like parchment, already old but looking a far older ruin than she was, she insisted upon her flatterers addressing her as though she were a woman of great beauty in the bloom of youth.

Elizabeth was never beautiful, and after the age of thirty she became repulsive. In that year she lost all her reddish hair through an illness and had to supply the loss by a reddish wig. Her complexion had never been good since the first years of her youth; but she carried herself with dignity and in spite of her physical disabilities her energy and vivacity of mind certainly made her a good companion. So far from her reign being the foundation of England's modern power or anything of that sort it was a period during which, as Thorold Rogers has proved, wealth was continually declining, towns shrinking in population and land going out of cultivation. It is true that a race of bold seamen arose contemporaneously with that reign, but they were no more remarkable than the captains of other nations in Europe at the same time and they nearly all bore the taint of theft and murder. They were slave-dealers and pirates, secretly supported by the powerful men of the State; Elizabeth could not but feel the shame which their piracies brought upon her in the eyes of her fellow sovereigns, and yet could not avoid taking part in the proceeds of the disgraceful business. For Cecil's principle was to let such men as Hawkins, Drake and the rest rob indiscriminately, to disavow them in public, to apologize for their acts, sometimes even to compensate the victims in part, but to keep the gains of their misdeeds—much the greater part of which went into the pockets of the men who held political power, while the criminal agents themselves were left with no more than a small commission. The only

military effort of the reign, that in Holland, was a ridiculous failure: the only effort at colonizaton was the equally ridiculous failure of Virginia.

In religion Elizabeth inclined at first to that witty, cynical skepticism of the Renaissance, the spirit of many intellectuals of the time in which she was steeped. She was ready in youth to adopt any outward conformity required of her. Calvinist as a girl, under the rule of those who were despoiling the State after her father's death, she was quite ready to profess enthusiasm for the Catholic Church, as we have seen, when her sister Mary was on the throne; but secretly enjoying the influence given her by the fact that the religious revolutionaries looked to her as a counterweight against her sister and as one who, when they could put her upon the throne, would make certain of their ill-gotten gains at the expense of the Catholic Church.

As she grew older she developed a certain measure of carefully concealed piety—her private prayers prove that. It is a feature not uncommon in people who are tortured by some abnormality in their intimate life. It is a sort of refuge for them.

Her mature sympathies were, of course, however vaguely, with the Catholic Church. All the great monarchs among whom she wished to be counted as an equal were struggling to maintain the old civilization of Europe, of which the Catholic faith was the creator and the supreme expression. Philip of Spain, the head of the Catholic movement, had saved her life; she had long respected and depended upon him until, in spite of her and in spite of himself, Cecil had turned him into an enemy. She tried hard for an understanding with the Papacy; she detested the new Anglican establishment which Cecil had put up and of which she was, in spite of herself, the political head.

It was one of those very few minor points on which she was allowed to have her own way that she refused to call herself as her father had called himself, "Vicar of Christ and Supreme Head of the Church on Earth." She detested the idea of a married clergy and always refused to receive the wives of the new Establishment. She would, had she been allowed, have sent emissaries to the Council of Trent; and though, of course, the thing cannot be proved and is pure conjecture, I have thought it certain enough that she would, in the case of a successful Catholic rising, had the Catholic emigrants and their supporters been able to bring a sufficient force into England, have joined what was still the religion of the majority of her subjects though cowed and terrorized by the reign of Cecil's government. The fall of that government would have been indeed a release for her.

As examples of the way in which she was "run" by those who were her masters, I will take four leading cases out of a very great number which might be quoted:

1. She had personally given her Royal assurance to the Spanish Minister that the Spanish treasure ships bearing the pay for Alva's soldiers in the Netherlands, the ships which had taken refuge from pirates in English harbours, should be released and the money taken under safeguards to its proper destination. Cecil simply overruled her. He ordered the money to be kept and confiscated in spite of her, and *his* orders, not *hers*, were obeyed.

2. Again, she desired to save Norfolk. Three separate times she interfered to prevent the execution. She was overruled. That unfortunate cousin of hers was put to death, but his blood is not upon her head; it is upon Cecil's.

3. She tried to recall Drake just before the open declaration of war with Spain; no one thought of obeying her orders in the matter.

4. The supreme example is the case of Mary, Queen of Scots. The murder—for it was a murder—was accomplished against her will. Our official historians have perpetually repeated that her agony at hearing of Mary's death was feigned: that is, false. It was genuine. The signing of the warrant had indeed been wrung out of her, but that did not mean that the warrant would be put into execution. It was put into execution in spite of her, in order that she should be made responsible, willing or unwilling,

One might add to the list at any length. Her paramour Leicester, did what he willed in Holland without consulting her, keeping a royal state which she flamed against impotently. Her later paramour, Essex, kept the loot of Cadiz and defied, without fear of consequences, her bitter anger at finding herself deprived of her royal right to the proceeds of an act of war undertaken in her name. She never desired the death of Essex; it was Robert Cecil, the second Cecil, who was responsible for Essex' death. Not only would she have prevented it if she could, but one may fairly say that she died of it.

And to what a death did the unhappy woman come! A death of madness and despair. The late Hugh Benson wrote a most powerful pamphlet contrasting that death with the holy, happy, and pious death of Mary.

She crouched on the ground for hours, one may say for days, refusing to speak, with her finger in her mouth, after having suffered horrible illusions—thinking that she had an iron band pressing round her head and on one occasion seeing herself in a sort of vision as a little figure surrounded with flames. She passed unannealed, unabsolved, and it is one of the most horrible stories in history.

Nevertheless we must admit her greatness. A warped, distorted, diseased greatness, but greatness nonetheless.

And there is another note on which I would conclude, a note of warning which is always necessary when one is correcting a false impression in history. The issue was not clear-cut. It must ever be so when the real power is in one hand, the nominal power in another. It is the nominal power which impresses men and even those who exercise the real power half believe in it, and those who exercise the nominal power also more than half believe in it. Cecil would never have told you that he was the real master of England, and, even though upon a strict examination of conscience he would have had to admit it, he still regarded himself a minister and servant. And she herself, Elizabeth, was of course filled with the idea of her office to the end, that ideal of monarchy which men still hold. Yet it was under her that the monarchy of England began to fall to pieces so rapidly that within half a lifetime after her death the rich taxpayers not only rose in rebellion successfully against the Crown, but put their monarch, her second successor, to death.

With that event, the beheading of Charles I, the old English monarchy came to an end, and it remained nothing but a simulacrum of itself. Government had passed to the gentry and to their two great committees, the House of Lords and the House of Commons.

Some day I suppose a true life of Elizabeth will be written in the English language, but, as I have said, we have not had it yet. There is here a great opportunity for the younger historians, and one of them I think will take it.

Sir John Neale

THE ELIZABETHAN AGE

Sir John Neale (1890-1976) until his death in 1976 was the dean of Tudor—especially Elizabethan—studies. Although Sir Lewis Namier's name has become associated with the "new" institutional history of the 1930s (which sought to view politics and institutions from the inside out—i.e., in terms of the interests, connections, and families of the individuals involved), John Neale developed a similar but less rigid approach to the study of Elizabeth's parliaments. His two-volume study, *Elizabeth I and Her Parliaments,* is a veritable gold mine of biographical and institutional history. Possibly no one, not even Froude, acquired a greater mastery or understanding of the documents of the age than did Neale; his biography of Elizabeth is a classic of literary style and historical scholarship. This Mandell Creighton Lecture—given in somewhat abbreviated form below —dramatizes not only the link between Bishop Creighton and John Neale, but also the position in which Great Britain found herself during the 1940s when, as in 1588, it seemed that she stood alone against the storm of ideological hysteria and aggression. The lecture

From Sir John E. Neale, *The Elizabethan Age* (Creighton Lecture in History, 1950, University of London), London: The Athlone Press, 1951, pp. 1-9, 14-21. Printed by permission of the publisher.

was delivered in 1951; the memory of Winston Churchill's leadership during World War II and the continued international tension associated with the Cold War were very much in Neale's mind when he sought to describe Elizabeth and her age in the light of historical perspective.

IT COULD hardly have been expected of me that I should choose any other subject for this occasion than my Elizabethan period; and the name of Bishop Creighton, whose work as a historian we commemorate, was also an injunction to keep to my last, for, as you all know, Creighton was one of Queen Elizabeth's biographers. There is, or there was, a tradition that this lecture should be broad in its scope (though not necessarily in its chronology); that it should proceed more obviously from reflection than from research. Seeking for a theme in this vein, it occurred to me that I might try to answer the question, What made the Elizabethan period a great age? Can the historian by his process of analysis answer, or at least throw some light on so subtle and difficult a question? If he can, then he may exceed the purely antiquarian purpose of satisfying man's curiosity about the past, and, in this bewildering, changing society of our own day, may proffer that modicum of understanding which is to be found in historical analogy. The supreme privilege of human beings among God's creatures is that they can garner experience; and history is man's storehouse.

No one is likely to accuse me of begging the question by assuming the greatness of the Elizabethan age. Its own people grew to be conscious of it. The ballad-writers, the chroniclers, the play-. wrights—in short, the literary voice of Elizabethan England, and voices abroad also, including Pope Sixtus V—proclaimed it. The apocalyptic mood of Mr. Churchill's great words—"This was their finest hour"—possessed many Elizabethans. And after the Queen was dead and the age become a memory, after the novelty of possessing a male

sovereign in the person of James I had worn off—and how quickly this happened!—Englishmen grasped with instinctive certainty that that indeed had been their finest hour. So the tradition remained in this land of ours. While personal monarchy lasted or religion suffused politics the greatness of the age was personified in Elizabeth....And when such passions died down and personal monarchy went out of fashion, still the age was acclaimed great, though the credit might be transferred from the sovereign to her ministers. In our own lifetime, even the cynics, in the years of disillusion after the first world war, however they bespattered personalities left the tradition about the age free from denigration.

Thus, with the consensus of the centuries behind us, we may proceed with our inquiry: Why did England achieve greatness in this age? If we try to generalize the question and apply it first to the individual, we might agree that in addition to the capacity for greatness there must be the will to achieve it and the opportunity. Many a potential genius must have died after a commonplace life through the lack of a chance to live otherwise; and all of us who have passed our youth must realize that opportunity may be there but ability alone is no guarantee that it will be seized. The same considerations surely hold in a nation's life. The thesis is implied in the passage of Mr. Churchill's from which I have already quoted. When the stream moves quietly and satisfactorily along, how tempting it is for a nation to rest on its oars!

In the Elizabethan period the waters were far from quiet. That, indeed, may partly explain why Elizabethan history has so manifest an appeal to readers today. Then, as now, Europe was concerned with the clash of two faiths inextricably mingled with politics. Then, as now, the devotees of both sides felt that the truth which was in them was a cause transcending all others. Do not be surprised that I compare the struggle of Catholicism and Protestantism in those days with that of our rival ideologies today. Time has detached religion from politics and emptied it of the old passion and intolerance: but sixteenth-century zealots viewed the rival faith with all the detestation and fear that we see in our world today; and the connection of religion with the state confused international and national politics....

The Elizabethan age opened with a striking victory for the Protestant revolution; and the subsequent events of the reign—the consolidation of the Catholic Church at the Council of Trent; the French Religious Wars with the infamous blood-bath of the Massacre of St. Bartholomew; the flight of Mary Queen of Scots to England, there to become the focus for religious and political discontent, leading almost immediately to the Rebellion of the North; the Papal Bull, releasing Englishmen from their allegiance to the Queen; the Papal plan of an "Enterprise" against Protestant England; the infiltration of Catholic missionaries from the continent, preparing, as it were, a "Fifth Column" for the day when the "Enterprise" would be launched; the recurrent plots against the Queen's throne and life; the unfolding of English policy as anti-Spanish and anti-Catholic—all these happenings, and more, determining the domestic and foreign climate of the next forty years, kept the spirit of revolution constantly alive, and as often as not at white-hot intensity.

Here we must note a paradox. The Queen herself had an instinctive hatred of revolution and its votaries. She did not want to proceed as rapidly as she was forced to do at the beginning of the reign; she modified the revolutionary Protes-

tant programme and injected conservative elements into the service and policy of the Anglican Church; throughout her reign she was the effective obstacle to Puritan activities; and time and again, with her caution and prudence and delays, she was the despair of her statesmen, carried away by the exuberance of the times. Nevertheless, even to the hotheads—indeed, to the hot-heads most of all— she was the personification of their cause. She was their Judith, their Deborah, their "Fayre Elisa, Queene of Shepheardes All," their Diana, their Laura, their "Cynthia, the Ladie of the Sea," their Gloriana and Belphoebe. These were not random extravagances, fashioned by Court sycophants. They voiced a national cult. An American scholar has made a meticulous study of the literature of the age and filled a substantial volume with extracts on such themes. Nor was literature the only expression of the mood. Running through the parliamentary debates of the reign, and reaching lyrical pitch during the period of plots and danger to Elizabeth's throne and life, is the same note. "If it might prolong her Majesty's life but for one year," said a Member in 1585, "I protest I would be content to suffer death with the most exquisite torments that might be devised." "It makes my heart leap for joy to think we have such a jewel," said another M.P.; "it makes my joints to tremble for fear, when I consider the loss of such a jewel." Both rhapsodists belonged to that large Puritan element in the House of Commons which managed to worship the Queen and yet be a never-ending source of trouble....

The cult of Elizabeth has its analogies with the cult of Mussolini, Hitler, and Stalin. It is interesting to reflect that nowadays the revolutionary *mystique* has had to find its personification in an individual, the head of the state, who in varying degree has been deified by its votaries. There are, however, profound differences to note, as well as analogies. The modern dictator finds the principal psychological basis of power in the cult of himself. He must be the high priest of the *mystique.*In the sixteenth century personal monarchy provided the framework for leadership: power rested on the office of monarch, and therefore it was possible for the Queen to personify the emotion of the nation without necessarily being doctrinaire. Hence the paradox of revolution with moderation at the helm.

Rare personal qualities, great art, and good fortune were needed for the role. It is said that no man can be a hero to his valet; but in this instance those about the sovereign had to be schooled into an instinctive recognition of leadership. A contemptuous, rotten, or merely *blasé* Court, though it attempted in its own sordid interests to sustain an artificial comedy, would have ruined the play. And there had to be the artistic capacity to draw out and respond to the emotion of the country at large. Elizabeth possessed these qualities *in excelsis*. But, as I have said, she was no revolutionary: she was not, as her sister, Mary Tudor, had been, a *dévote*. Good fortune—which was partly policy—also enters into the argument. If Elizabeth had had a husband and family, the chances are that the ardours of English Puritans would have found a rival focus and their discontents have been directed against the sovereign, thus destroying the spell over the community. In quite another way than that usually thought of, a Virgin Queen may have been essential to the Elizabethan tradition.

Elizabethan England should be regarded as a revolutionary age: that is the point I am anxious to make. Hitler claimed that a nation so inspired is irresistible, except by a like faith. And though Hitler's Germany was overwhelmed, this was accomplished by an opposing faith, stronger for being detached from fanaticism. Indeed, the boast was not an empty one. Inspiration, a sense of purpose, faith, and enthusiasm: though we may sometimes think them misplaced, devilish, or what you will, are they not ingredients of greatness? And surely they are qualities which we perceive in many aspects of the Elizabethan age. They were present in a strange blend of lust for easy riches, piratical impulse, patriotism, and fervid Protestant zeal in the voyages of Elizabethan seamen....Listen to the mystical note in the writing of John Davys, the Elizabethan navigator:

There is no doubt but that we of England are this saved people, by the eternal and infallible presence of the Lord predestinated to be sent unto these Gentiles in the sea, to those Isles and famous Kingdoms, there to preach the peace of the Lord: for are not we only set upon Mount Zion to give light to all the rest of the world? Have not we the true handmaid of the Lord to rule us, unto whom the eternal majesty of God hath revealed his truth and supreme power of Excellency?...It is only we, therefore, that must be these shining messengers of the Lord, and none but we....

But behind this *mystique* what was there? Certainly not a propaganda machine, nor a police state. There was a society which politically, socially, and economically had many reasons, if not every reason, to be buoyant. This was the culminating period or phase of a civilization, in which conservative elements from the past were still a vigorous reality, while new forces, having overcome an initial extravagance, had not yet developed their inner weaknesses to the point of gross abuse and social collapse....

Within forty years of Elizabeth's death, after almost as many years of increasing political, religious, and social discontent, England was rent by civil war. The political machine had broken down. That fact alone would prompt us to ask how intimate was the connection between the greatness of the age that was past and its system of government. The answer will be clearer if we first draw a moral or two from the Stuart tragedy. When Elizabeth died, the Tudor political system was doomed.... The only question was whether there would be imaginative and peaceful adaptation to a new age or whether incompetent leadership would allow the old system to fester and collapse. James I succeeded to an impoverished crown: he cannot be blamed on that count. He was weak in character, and did not know when to say "No": these are fatal defects in any leader. He subjected Court and government to favourites, and between them they allowed the mercenary instincts of individuals free play. Corruption was rampant, honour cheapened by the sale of peerages and lesser dignities. The political and social evils, evident in the England of 1603, grew like deadly weeds; and, as the dramatists of the time perceived, the decencies of the old order were violated. Charles I completed the disaster. He turned the Puritans and the House of Commons, who had been the most ardent of Queen Elizabeth's votaries, into dangerous critics of the monarchy. Instead of personifying a nation, he led a party.

Control was what the nation needed, and what it got in the reign of Elizabeth; control which, while encouraging the energies of the people and sustaining their gaiety, restrained the cruder promptings of individualism. Government was paternal; and in the economic sphere I fancy we should understand it better if we compared it with the present-day regulated State with its emphasis on the public good. Everything depended from the centre. All aspects of life, from the personal behaviour of individuals to high matters of state came before either the Crown or the Council, or both. And never before and never again was the Privy Council so efficient. Elizabeth kept it small, balancing extremely able commoners with aristocrats; and even the aristocrats were converted by hard work and good training into tolerable and sometimes highly effective statesmen. Unlike James I, she did not blur the distinction between the two elements by rewarding the commoners with peerages.

William Cecil was the signal exception to this policy, which maintained the professional outlook of the abler administrators.

But the sovereign was even more important than the Council in determining the quality of government. Under personal monarchy the machinery of government was the ruler's. In theory it was intimately linked with the royal prerogative, while in practice there was a flexibility which permitted and even demanded constant intervention from the center....Elizabeth was perfunctory about nothing. Or to be precise, her officials could never rely upon her being perfunctory: which had much the same result. They could never be sure of obtaining her signature to a document without an inquisition, followed sometimes by biting criticism and a stormy refusal. She might interfere in anything...."I would to God," wrote Walsingham on one occasion, when she criticized the phrasing and latinity of the commission to try Mary Queen of Scots,"her Majesty could be content to refer these things to them that can best judge of them, as other princes do."...

The effect of such a person in such a position was to keep faction, corruption, and other abuses in check, and to maintain that order of "degree, priority, and place" which was the fragrant essence of society. The able men she chose as her statesmen, and particularly William Cecil, by their vigilance and hard work helped to made a success of paternal government.

It was the Queen herself who kept the nation charged with emotion. The citizens of London and the multitude of visitors there were thrilled by their frequent sight of her. In later life Bishop Goodman described how when a boy in the year 1588, on a dark December evening, they were suddenly told that the Queen was gone to council,"and if you will see the Queen you must come quickly." They ran to Whitehall and were admitted to the courtyard, which, lighted by torches, was soon full. After an hour's wait, they saw Elizabeth emerge, "in great state."

Then we cried "God save your Majesty! God save your Majesty!" Then the Queen turned unto us and said, "God bless you all, my good people!" Then we cried again "God save your Majesty! God save your Majesty!" Then the Queen said again unto us, "You may well have a greater prince, but you shall never have a more loving prince." And so, looking one upon another awhile, the Queen departed. This wrought such an impression upon us, for shows and pageants are ever best seen by torch-light, that all the way long we did nothing but talk what an admirable queen she was, and how we would adventure our lives to do her service.

The countryside was given a taste of Londoners' ecstasy in the Queen's annual progresses.

Or take an illustration of the personal touch in quite different style: her treatment of Drake when, at a most delicate and threatening moment in Anglo-Spanish relations, he returned from his voyage round the world. His plunder had to be sequestered in case Elizabeth was compelled to return it; but she sent word that he was to be allowed, in utmost secrecy, to abstract ten thousand pounds' worth of it. She received him at Court, listened with delight to his story, and made her celebrated visit to Deptford to knight him aboard the *Golden Hind*. One might say that she had cocked a snook at Philip of Spain. At such a critical time it was impudent bravura; but it was also political art. As for her skill in handling Parliament—her supreme achievement in patriotic romance—that is a story which would be credible only if fully told.

And now, perhaps, we can assemble our argument. The Elizabethan age was one of rapidly expanding horizons, economic, cultural, and geographical; an age to stir the imagination and incite the energies of the people. At Court, the structure of politics, based on faction and emulation, kept life intense and vigorous. Though sordid in many of its details, it was transformed into romance by the personality of the Queen and disciplined by her masterful character, backed by an acute and highly trained intelligence. In the country the day of the gentry had arrived. It was not simply a matter of inheriting and maintaining old standards of wealth and comfort. Life was in flux: a challenge to enterprise and ability. As at Court, faction and rivalry stirred and invigorated county society. At times and places they revealed their evil side, but they were kept within bounds by the aristocratic structure of society— that doctrine of "degree, priority, and place"—and by the vigilant authority of the Privy Council. In the towns, Fortune could be wooed, and for the ambitious apprentice there were success stories, such as that of Jack of Newbury, which sober life did not render incredible: stories which might be likened to the proverbial marshal's baton for the Napoleonic soldier, or "From Log Cabin to White House" for the American of half a century or more ago....

Consider the impact on such a society of those voyages whose narratives Hakluyt collected, with their stories and fables of new-found lands and peoples. To a youthful and responsive age, sure of the verbal inspiration of the Bible, conscious of divine intervention in the triumphs and afflictions of everyday life, and believing the many tales of monstrous births and miraculous happenings which honest John Stow recorded in his *Chronicles* and ballad-makers sometimes commemorated in verse—to such an age stories from afar were merely an extension of the wonders in an illimitable world. "All things became possible; credulity was wiser than experience."...

Government, I am convinced, was a principal, if not the principal ingredient of national greatness. Would all that energy have been released if the political setting had been different?... Then, it is obvious that the story of voyage and exploration would have been different if Mary Tudor had lived to old age and Philip of Spain remained King of England. Supposing, however, that there had been a regime, similar to the Elizabethan in religious and constitutional complexion but less efficient and less inspiring. What then? Political, religious, and social discontent would have emerged sooner; and even if the friction thus created had not hindered the growth of wealth and enterprise, it would have emptied national life of its spirit. Instead of living in the present, men might have looked to the past—to the days of Bluff King Hal, as Jacobeans looked to the days of Good Queen Bess. Instead of "a literature of youth and hope," there might have been "a literature of regret and memory." England was a small community— four to five millions, knit together socially in many ways, some of which I have described. What wireless has done for our generation, the size, homogeneity, and cohesion of Elizabethan society did for those days. It made romantic leadership of the nation possible. If, in sober historical documents no less than in the literature of the age, the emotional tie of sovereign and people is abundantly clear, then surely it is no illusion to imagine that such leadership enabled the nation to achieve its "finest hour." After all, we have lived through a similar period ourselves.

Lacey Baldwin Smith

ELIZABETH TUDOR: PORTRAIT OF A QUEEN

Lacey Baldwin Smith, currently a professor of history at Northwestern University, belongs to that school of history which seeks to relate action—both individual and collective—to the cultural and intellectual premises and subliminal assumptions of a particular society, as well as to see institutions as collections of individuals and not as corporate or constitutional entities in their own rights. Smith's name is usually associated with the earlier period of Tudor history, for he has written a group analysis of the Henrician bishops, *Tudor Prelates and Politics, 1536-1558,* and a psychohistorical biography of the second Tudor, *Henry VIII, the Mask of Royalty.* But he has also written *The Elizabethan World,* a study of the Elizabethan era in its European context and a short biography entitled *Elizabeth Tudor: Portrait of a Queen.* The latter study, from which this selection comes, is an essay on the nature of political power in Tudor England, and how it was exercised by a woman in a man's world.

From *Elizabeth Tudor: Portrait of a Queen* by Lacey Baldwin Smith, pp. 73-77, 214-218. Copyright© 1975 by Lacey Baldwin Smith. Reprinted by permission of Little, Brown and Company.

How DID she do it? How did she end as she began with her subjects' love? It is easy to dismiss the mystery and say Englishmen had no choice; they had to make do with Elizabeth because fate had left them only a capricious idol before whom to bend the knee. Had Gloriana not existed, it would have been necessary to create her in a beleaguered kingdom desperate for a human symbol of spiritual and political unity, conditioned to believe that God spoke directly through kings, and instinctively aware that the natural leaders of a hierarchic structure could exercise authority over inferiors only if they themselves were obedient to a higher power. It was an axiom of sixteenth-century political life that "fear of some divine and supreme power keeps men in obedience," and Tudor society was fully aware that there was a secret mystery in "the pompous pride of state and dignity." Atavistic fear of the divinity that encased the throne with the aura of God's special protection and the potent memory of Henry VIII's majesty restrained the hand of William Parry, who had determined to assassinate the Queen but "was so daunted with the majesty of her presence" in which he perceived the image of her father "that his heart would not suffer his hand to execute that which he had resolved." Fear that paralyzed the hand and state pageantry that befuddled the eye are, however, insufficient explanations of what was in essence a "mystical phenomenon." The true subject did not need the gruesome spectacle of disembowelment or the church's fervent assurance of a warm welcome in hell to propel him along the path of obedience. Gloriana's safety lay neither in the sword nor in elaborate, outward obeisance but in the love and loyalty that wished her well with "heart and mind."

Obedience is a two-way proposition —the willingness to accept orders and the confidence that they will be carried out—and effective power requires careful mental conditioning on the part of both the giver and the receiver. Fortunately for Elizabeth her subjects in 1558 shared their Queen's lofty view of her high office, and though they grumbled and complained like restless and aggrieved schoolchildren, they accepted the scolding of their royal nanny as part of the natural order of things. Subjects saw her as she so often saw herself— "She is our God in earth. If there be perfection in flesh and blood, undoubtedly it is in her Majesty." The conditional, nature of the eulogy was necessary to a society as sensible of the realities of human imperfection as it was hierarchical in its thinking. Sir Francis Knollys, on the other hand, good Puritan though he was, attached no strings to his acceptance of his Queen's prerogative: what "secret cause or scruple there may be in the hearts of princes, it is not for all people to know"; and William Cecil in terms both touching and convincing expressed the creed of unswerving obedience that a servant owed his master: "As long as I may be allowed to give advice, I will not change my opinion by affirming the contrary, for that were to offend God, to whom I am sworn first; but as a servant I will obey her Majesty's commandment...presuming that she being God's chief minister here, it shall be God's will to have her commandments obeyed...and shall in my heart wish her commandments to have such good success as I am sure she intendeth."

Absolute confidence in an idol who had, after all, alarming human characteristics was made more palatable by that political principle which was in part mental reflex and in part deliberate conspiracy: the myth of the evil adviser. Critics of the crown's policies and victims of the Queen's less pleasant personal qualities were afforded an outlet for their anger and frustration. In 1587 Essex was confronted with overwhelming evidence of Gloriana's vindictive pettiness. The Earl's sister, Dorothy Devereux, had married without royal or parental consent. When the Queen arrived on prog-

ruderers, boldness

ress at the residence of the Earl of Warwick she discovered that Dorothy was
also a guest, and promptly ordered her to
be confined to her room. It was done for
spite and to enrage Essex, for Elizabeth
had been forewarned by Essex himself of
his sister's presence and could easily
have avoided an embarrassing confrontation. The Earl was furious at what he
rightly construed to be a public slight to
his family honor, but his handling of the
affair is sociologically significant. Instead of accusing Elizabeth of outright
nastiness and provocation, he jumped to
the conclusion that his archrival at court,
Sir Walter Raleigh, had poisoned the
Queen's mind, toyed with her womanly
affection and persuaded her to insult him
"in the eyes of the world."

Elizabeth's reputation remained intact, but the creed that a monarch could
do no wrong had its price; to sustain the
myth, royalty on occasion had to be
turned into a sponge of incompetence,
continually absorbing sinister advice.
The legend of Henry VIII's Bacchana-
lian revelry stemmed in part from the
need to explain and justify evil actions,
and with considerable political acumen
but little historic justice, the Vicar of
Eastbourne exempted his sovereign from
all responsibility for the new religious
policies of his reign on the grounds that
"they that rule about the King make him
great banquets and give him sweet wines
and make him drunk, and then they bring
him bills and he putteth his sign to
them." Under Elizabeth there were no
grounds for blaming that devil drink; nor
was there need: she was a woman and
by definition weak, frail, impatient, feeble and "void of the spirit of council."
She was, as the Spanish Ambassador not
very tactfully put it, "only a passionate,
ill-advised woman." Although Elizabeth
enjoyed the imputation of incompetence no more than her father had, there
were compensations for being "a virgin
prince." She was able to indulge her desire to be hateful without tarnishing her
public image. "Her sex," remarked one

of the less sympathetic observers of the
court, "did bear out many impertinences
in her words and actions."

If the fiction of royalty's perfection
was to be made a political reality it was
essential to divorce the crown from the
uglier aspects of power. Kings were the
fountain of every man's expectations and
they could not be found denying a
patron-seeker, refusing a pardon, making
a wrong decision or levying a burden-
some tax. There must always be a
scapegoat to absorb the filth of partisan
politics, and by Elizabeth's reign the
function of a second, political king was
clearly understood in practice if not in
theory. William Cecil was accused of
operating a *regnum Cecilianum,* but the
Queen's minister dismissed the title as
malicious mockery and ruefully explained the true nature of his rule. "True
it is," he lamented, "that her Majesty
throweth upon me a burden to deal in all
ungrateful actions—to give answers unpleasant to suitors that miss....My burden also is this that in all suits for lands,
leases and such things, her Majesty commands me to certify the state thereof....And if the party obtain [the grant], I
am not thanked; if not, the fault (though
false) is imputed to me." Elizabeth took
every advantage of the system. As Sir
John Harington said, "She did most cun-
ningly commit the good issue to her own
honour and understanding; but when
aught fell out contrary to her will and
intent, the Council were in great straits to
defend their own acting and not blemish
the Queen's good judgment." In desper-
ation Cecil wrote to Walsingham in November of 1588 that "all irresolutions
and lacks are thrown upon us two. The
wrong is intolerable." The system may
have been personally unjust but it was
politically necessary, and Cecil sadly acknowledged that the world would always
blame the "lacks and errors to some of us
that are accounted inward Councillors,
where indeed the fault is not," but "they
must be so suffered and imputed for saving the honour of the highest."

being charged w/incompetance

Gloriana Bess ↘ other names

Elizabeth made no distinctions between great and small. Burghley was her "spirit" and Essex her "wildhorse," but on progress to Warwick she thanked the town recorder for his speech of welcome in words just as artful as those usually reserved for lords of great estate. "Come hither, little Recorder. They told me you would be afraid to look upon me or to speak boldly. But you were not so much afraid of me as I was of you!" The theatrical sham is overwhelming: the conceit of Gloriana telling her kingdom that she was more afraid of a small-town functionary than he was of her. Yet in the midst of the preposterous was a tiny fragment of truth. It was not so much that Bess was endowed with true humility as that she never allowed power to corrupt either her judgment or her compassion. She was a ruthless and calculating political egotist and she demanded unconditional surrender which, as Essex discovered, no amount of ingrained deference to authority, political connivance or respect for a magnificent performance could make entirely palatable, but Elizabeth possessed one feature which redeemed all else—she knew herself for what she was. Juno was "no angel," and she confessed that she might be "unworthy of eternal life, if not of royal dignity." The distinction was important, for unlike her father Elizabeth kept a firm hold upon reality. Her conscience never fell victim to the theatrical deception of her office or became the servant of expediency. She knew she was "a most frail substance" surrounded by a "world of wickedness, where delights be snares." She accepted her royal status as a marvelous dignity, but she also assured her people after forty-three years of benevolent despotism "that the shining glory of princely authority hath not so dazzled the eyes of our understanding, but that we will know and remember that we also are to yield an account of our actions before the Great Judge."

Gloriana moved in a world of appearances and deceptions where it was "more important to seem than to be"; behind the self-absorption, however, lay something more than empty desire for power. She never forgot that she had once been a subject, fearful and defenseless like her little Recorder. Her vision could always accommodate others, and as a consequence almost no one on whom she relied ever betrayed her. Elizabeth sensed that her ablest ministers were not without their pettiness and that "the greatest clerks are not always the wisest men." All her reign she had been surrounded by flatterers, self-seekers and fanatics, every bit as greedy for ransom and power as in the days of Somerset and Northumberland. Courtiers, as Sir Francis Bacon warned, were constantly spying into her "humours and conceits" to "second them, and not only second them, but in seconding increase them." Yet Elizabeth somehow managed to see through the deceit: "I perceive they dealt with me like physicians who, ministering a drug, make it more acceptable by giving it a good aromatical savour, or when they give pills do gild them all over."

It takes a thief to catch a thief, and none could gild a pill better than the Queen, but the explanation of her extraordinary hold over those who suffered her lashing tongue and caustic wit goes deeper than theatrics. Her goals were not very lofty—security and quiet for herself and her kingdom so that both could enjoy the pleasant gifts that God had bestowed—but she was one of those rare rulers who anguished over means and ends and who perceived that the substance of policy is more enduring than either the language in which it is wrapped or the ideological form it assumes. Living in a century of domestic and international hypertension, she was content, as she had told Parliament, "to defer, but not reject." She saw that the quarrels that divided men and kingdoms were almost never resolved by force or policy, but were simply set aside and forgotten, replaced by more pressing and popular issues.

The very quality which infuriated Elizabeth's devoted councillors the most was, in fact, her saving grace. She might, as Raleigh said, do "all things by halves," and Sir Thomas Smith might "have somewhat ado...to get anything signed," but neither Raleigh nor Smith faced the responsibilities of an office in which sovereigns had not only to live with their decisions but to die with them as well; as the Venetian Ambassador said early in the reign, "Queen Elizabeth... declines to rely on anyone save herself, though she is most gracious to all." Both Bess and her father hated the burden of ultimate responsibility. Henry developed his own defense mechanisms, but Gloriana was satisfied with delay. She stayed the execution of the Duke of Norfolk for months because, as she told William Cecil, "the causes that move me to this are not now to be expressed, lest an irrevocable deed be in meanwhile committed." Her judgment was divine, and even at the cost of procrastination, missed chances and half-measures, it had to be protected from both human error and the arbitrary rule of men. Doubt in a divine-right monarch is a corroding disease, for it strikes at God Himself. Henry VIII sought to protect himself by never changing his mind once he had come to a decision, for those who are filled with the spirit of divinity cannot forever be shifting their grounds. Elizabeth shielded herself as far as she could by never making a decision, or at least never making one which was irrevocable.

Unlike her father, Gloriana had a marvelous sense of means commensurate to ends. She hated to use an ax where the surgeon's blade would do, for she preferred the patient to live; a mutilated corpse could neither pay taxes nor give good service. This was why Essex' death was such a shock. Her ministers often complained that her means, or the lack thereof, were insufficient to her political purpose; that either more doctors were needed to keep the patient alive, or more surgeons required to remove the diseased member or more blood necessary to purge the body politic. Her procrastination tended to become habitual with age, but in truth it had been forced upon her from the start, for Elizabeth was a monarch who was continually at odds with her Council over both the style and the purpose of state policy. Without an outright confrontation delay was often her sole recourse. Postponement was the only way Elizabeth could exercise control in a world filled with activist, military men and enthusiasts who displayed immaculate logic and highest motives but were devoid of humor or doubt.

Though her ends were the selfish product of her father's outmoded monarchy and of an egotism which found satisfaction in the applause accorded fine showmanship and the deference given to high office, Elizabeth never approached matters of life and death from the threadbare perspective of statistics, ideology or *raison d'état*. Ends, even those involving her priceless legitimacy and divinity, never totally justified the means, because Gloriana saw policy in terms of human beings, not abstractions. She possessed two sensitive and highly developed political attributes which were guaranteed to blunt the edge of tyranny—the ability to empathize, to place herself in the shoes of others, and the willingness to ask herself the one question that could curb the despotism of ideas: what if I am wrong? Though she spoke for God, Elizabeth knew that she was only human, and she never forgot what she had told a deeply concerned Parliament after her recovery from smallpox in 1563: "I know now as well as I did before that I am mortal. I know also that I must seek to discharge myself of that great burden that God hath laid upon me." The essence of that burden and the indispensable quality of her style of rule was the realization that, though protocol and law were essential to authority, government entailed more than the precise enforcement of rigid principles. The substance of

the way something gets done to get results.

justice had to encompass the individual. Against those fervent disciples of state and divine justice who wished her to be done with Mary of Scotland, Elizabeth gave an answer which is worth recording—"You lawyers are so nice and so precise in shifting and scanning every word and letter, that many times you stand more upon form than matter, upon syllables than the sense of the law." No matter how sterile and institutionalized her rule eventually became or how much a younger generation might wish their "dread sovereign" gone, her godson John Harington voiced the verdict of all who had enjoyed her rule for almost half a century when he said, "I shall not hastily put forth for a new master."

CONCLUSION

ASCINATION with Elizabeth has been endless and without restraint. Her sex life has been scrutinized, her medical problems inspected, her girlhood involvements probed, and her speeches analyzed; it has even been suggested that she was Shakespeare. The only approach lacking is a full–scale psychiatric study. The price of fame, it would appear, is that nothing is sacred; yet the riddle of Elizabeth's success remains essentially unresolved, and over the centuries historians and theologians, critics and admirers, professionals and amateurs have gone back to the source of the mystery—the woman herself. The mark of greatness may not lie solely in originality of mind or consequences of actions, but rather in complexity of character and juxtaposition of personality to time and place. There are at least sixty biographies of Elizabeth, and each writer, each generation, each century has found something different to praise, ask, or criticize about the Queen. Was she a good woman but a bad monarch, or conversely a horrid human being but a splendid sovereign? Was she the victim of her advisers, managed without knowing it by men and women wiser than herself, or did she in fact decide policy and manipulate events and actions without fanfare or staging? Was she supremely lucky, or was she incredibly adroit? Did she really care for Robert Dudley, Robert Devereux, Walter Raleigh, and the other butterflies of the court, or did she simply toy with them? Was she a victim of passion, emotion and fear, or was she like a goddess, always in control of herself and those around her? Was she only a soulless but splendid actress who knew how to put on a spectacular show, craving the flattery of her admirers and delighting in the knowledge that she could do with her audience what she pleased? And finally, what role, if any, did she play in creating that environment that produced Thomas Marlowe and William Shakespeare, Francis Drake and Walter Raleigh, William Harvey and Francis Bacon, Edmund Spenser and Philip Sidney?

The seventeenth century of necessity was cautious in its estimation of Elizabeth, for it suffered the rule of the son, grandson, and great–grandsons of the woman whom Gloriana put to death to save her own life, and it had to live with the consequences of the Queen's refusal to adapt her government to the changing realities of life. Indeed, it was Edward Hyde, Earl of Clarendon, who lived through the Civil War and wrote *The History of the Great Rebellion,* that saw beyond the myth of the Elizabethan past to the unpleasant realities of her reign. He noted "the charge, trouble and anxiety" of prolonged international war, chronic treason at home, constant "apprehension of what was to come," and the "unparalleled act of blood upon the life of a crowned neighbour, queen and ally," and he concluded that these tribulations of Elizabeth's reign "clouded much of that prosperity" which "now shines with so much splendour before our eyes in the chronicle." By the eighteenth century, however, Elizabeth had become the embodiment of the enlightened monarch who, in the words of David Hume's *History of England*, "by the force of her mind...controlled all her more active and stronger qualities and prevented them from running into excess." But it was the nineteenth century that struggled hardest with Gloriana; clearly magnificent and marvelous things had happened during her reign but, unfortunately, the more that nineteenth-century historians studied the Queen, the more evidence they uncovered that she was a complete autocrat who had small regard for that jewel of British constitutional history—Parliament—and who appeared to be both niggardly in finance and devoid of any real religious emotion. Thomas Macaulay and Anthony Froude, for example, both had difficulty reaching conclusions about Elizabeth. Each had grown up on the legend of her reign, of a "golden age" when the roots of empire, naval supremacy, and constitutional government emerged. "Surely," concluded Macaulay, "she was a great woman." But Anthony Froude was not totally convinced, as we have seen. By the time the twentieth century dawned and historians began to experience for themselves the consequences of ideological war, scholars were more willing to applaud Elizabeth's concern for economy and her lack of religious conviction. They were also more interested in the techniques of her leadership than in passing moral judgment on her character. The twentieth century, with its obsession for management, organization, chain-of-command, and the operation of power, has found in Elizabeth I an irresistible study in the metaphysics of political success.

SUGGESTIONS FOR ADDITIONAL READING

The best modern full scale study remains that classic of historical biography, Sir John Neale's *Queen Elizabeth* (London, 1934; paperback 1957). Elizabeth emerges as a heroine at whose feet Sir John is happy to worship. More technical but more revealing of her political finesse and skill is his two–volume analysis of *Elizabeth I and Her Parliaments* (London, 1953, 1957). Since Sir John's "romance" with Gloriana back in 1934, biographers have been pouring forth at a rate of almost one a year. Mary M. Luke's two volumes—*A Crown for Elizabeth* (New York, 1970) and *Gloriana: The Years of Elizabeth I* (New York, 1973)—are highly readable; Neville Williams, *Elizabeth the First, Queen of England* (New York, 1968) is the work of an able scholar; Paul Johnson, *Elizabeth I, a Study in Power and Intellect* (London, 1974) reflects, as its title indicates, the direction of modern interest; and Elizabeth Jenkins, *Elizabeth the Great* (New York, 1959) is the closest thing to a psychological study of the Queen available. Lacey B. Smith, *Elizabeth Tudor: Portrait of a Queen* (Boston, 1975) is not a full–length biography but an essay on the exercise of power by a woman in a man's world.

The moment the reader seeks to expand the perspective to include the circle of the Queen's contemporaries and the environment in which they operated, the selection becomes incredibly rich, for some of the best modern scholarship in English history is being done on the Tudor period. Lawrence Stone, *The Crisis of the Aristocracy 1558-1641* (Oxford, 1965) is a profound sociological analysis of the ruling elite; Wallace Mac-Caffrey, *The Shaping of the Elizabethan Regime* (Princeton, 1968; paperback 1971) is a gem of synthesizing the events of the first decade of the reign; A.L. Rowse, *The England of Elizabeth* (London, 1951) is a fine portrait of the age; Garrett Mattingly, *The Defeat of the Spanish Armada* (London, 1959) is a historical masterpiece; and E.M.W. Tillyard, *The Elizabethan World Picture* (London, 1943) is an intellectual *tour de force*. The Queen's Irish wars can be studied in Cyril Falls, *Elizabeth's Irish Wars* (London, 1950); the religious crisis is handled from varying perspectives by A.G. Dickens, *The English Reformation* (New York, 1964), Patric Collinson, *The Elizabethan Puritan Movement* (Berkeley, 1967), and Philip Hughes, *The Reformation in England,* 3 vols. (London, 1950-1954). The imperial profile is best read in J. A. Williamson, *The Age of Drake* (London, 1938) and *Sir John Hawkins* (Oxford, 1927). Anthony Esler has written a provocative generational study entitled, *The Aspiring Mind of the Elizabethan Younger Generation* (Durham, 1966).

As for those contemporaries who helped to shape the Queen's personality and influence her reign, it is surprising that there is no definitive study of her mother—Anne Boleyn—although Hester Chapman, *Anne Boleyn* (London, 1974) has made a start. Her father's first wife, Catherine of Aragon, has received scholarly if kind handling by Garrett Mattingly (Boston, 1941). The biographies of Henry VIII are legion. The best history of the reign is Jack Scarisbrick, *Henry VIII* (Berkeley, 1968), and the works on Henry most useful for understanding Elizabeth are Lacey B. Smith, *Henry VIII, the Mask of Royalty* (Boston, 1968) and A. F. Pollard, *Henry VIII* (London, 1902). Edward VI's short reign has been fully treated by W. K. Jordan, *Edward VI: The Young King* (Cambrige,1968) and *Edward VI: The Threshold of Power* (Cambridge, 1970). H. F. M. Prescott, *Mary Tudor* (New York, 1953) is still the best study of Elizabeth's sister, and Antonia Fraser's *Mary Queen of Scots* (London, 1969) is a careful although partisan account of that difficult lady. William Cecil has received his just deserts in Conyers Read's thorough but ponderous two-volume biography, *Mr. Secretary Cecil and Queen Elizabeth* (London, 1955) and *Lord Burghley and Queen Elizabeth* (London, 1960). Robert Dudley, Earl of Leicester, still awaits his scholarly biography, but the reader might want to try Elizabeth Jenkins, *Elizabeth and Leicester* (New York, 1962). Essex has been treated with sensitivity and perception by Robert Lacey, *Robert, Earl of Essex: An Elizabethan Icarus* (London, 1971), and Sir Walter Raleigh has been studied from a multitude of angles in W. M. Wallace, *Sir Walter Raleigh* (Princeton, 1959); Robert Lacey, *Sir Walter Raleigh* (New York, 1974); and Stephen J. Greenblatt, *Sir Walter Raleigh: The Renaissance Man and His Roles* (New Haven, 1973). Finally, old Lord Burghley's son, Robert Cecil, who dominated the final years of the reign and engineered the peaceful succession of James I, can be studied in P. M. Handover, *The Second Cecil* (London, 1959).

The list is endless; its extent and degree of detail can be seen in Conyers Read, *Bibliography of British History: The Tudor Period* (Oxford, 1959), which records some 6,543 entries, and Mortimer Levine's shorter and more modern compilation, *Tudor England, 1485-1603* (Cambridge, England, 1968).